MEDITATIⵑNS
WITH CROWS

Messages from the Corvid Realm

D.R. T STEPHENS

S.D.N Publishing

CONTENTS

CHAPTER 1:
INTRODUCTION
TO THE MYSTICAL
WORLD OF CORVIDS

1.1 UNVEILING THE MYSTERY

Few animals have captured human imagination as thoroughly as the crow and its relatives in the corvid family. Whether you've seen them perched solemnly on a branch, witnessed their playful antics, or heard their complex vocalizations, it's likely that these birds have piqued your curiosity in one way or another. What you might not realize, however, is that the fascination with corvids is not a modern phenomenon—it's as old as civilization itself.

Throughout history, crows and their corvid kin have been subjects of myths, legends, and folklore. In Norse mythology, for instance, Odin, the god of wisdom and war, had two ravens named Huginn and Muninn who served as his eyes and ears, flying across the world to bring back news. In Native American folklore, the crow is often portrayed as a trickster figure, a creature of intelligence and cunning. In Celtic traditions, crows are associated with Morrigan, the goddess of war and fate, embodying both life and death. Whether seen as omens of change or creatures with magical qualities, the roles crows play in mythology are both diverse and profound.

Even beyond myth, crows hold cultural significance around the globe. In Japan, the crow is revered as a divine messenger, while in some parts of Africa, they're seen as a symbol of fertility and abundance. From Australian Aboriginal stories to Russian folktales, these birds recur in narratives that suggest an enduring relationship between humans and corvids—one that transcends geographic and cultural boundaries.

Interestingly, this mystical view of crows and corvids doesn't stand in opposition to scientific knowledge; rather, it complements it. Research in the field of animal cognition has illuminated the corvid family as one of the most intelligent bird groups. Multiple studies have confirmed that some corvid species exhibit behaviors akin to problem-solving, self-awareness, and even planning for the future. These intellectual capacities not only rival those of many mammals but also challenge our understanding of intelligence itself.

But what does it mean for us today? How do we marry these two worlds—the scientific and the mystical—to deepen our understanding of these enigmatic birds? The answer may lie in looking beyond what we see on the surface and venturing into the meditative and spiritual dimensions that corvids offer. By harmonizing scientific insights with the spiritual wisdom encoded in our myths and traditions, we can forge a more enriching, nuanced relationship with these remarkable birds.

As you journey through this book, you'll discover that the world of crows is not merely one of black feathers and cawing calls but a realm rich in symbolism, layered with meaning, and teeming with lessons that can enhance our own lives. You'll learn about the intricate social dynamics of these birds, their astonishing cognitive abilities, and their significant roles in myths and contemporary culture. Perhaps most importantly, you'll be invited to explore various avenues for connecting with crows on a deeply spiritual level through meditative practices.

In this complex tapestry where science meets spirituality, you'll find that crows are not just passive creatures to be observed but active participants in a dialogue that has the potential to transform how we see the world and our place in it. So, let us embark on this fascinating exploration, unfolding the manifold layers that constitute the intriguing realm of corvids.

1.2 SCIENTIFIC PERSPECTIVE

As we traverse the corridors of myths and folklore that have long shaped our understanding of crows and their corvid relatives, it's equally vital to illuminate the pathways lit by scientific research. Science offers us rigorous tools to explore the intelligence, cognition, and behaviors of these enigmatic birds, giving us nuanced perspectives that enrich our interactions with them. The aim of this chapter is to present what modern science reveals about corvid intelligence and cognition, thereby harmonizing the mystical allure with empirical evidence.

Cognitive Abilities

Corvids, especially crows and ravens, have been the focus of numerous studies investigating animal cognition. The term "cognition" refers to the mental processes involved in acquiring knowledge and understanding through thought, experience, and the senses. One of the most fascinating aspects of corvid cognition is their problem-solving ability. Experiments have shown that crows can use tools to extract insects from tight spaces, a behavior traditionally associated with primates. Even more remarkably, some crows have been observed to craft their own tools—a feature that places them in a small, elite group of animals that use objects in a way that involves forward planning.

Social Complexity

The social structure of corvids is complex and highly organized. Studies reveal that these birds engage in cooperative behavior, often working together to achieve common goals like food gathering or predator deterrence. Their social interactions are not limited to their own species; crows and ravens are known to form associations with larger animals like wolves, following them to scavenge the remains of their hunts. This shows not just social awareness but also a capacity for interspecies communication.

Communication Skills

Speaking of communication, research has identified a multitude of vocalizations in crows that serve different purposes. These range from warning calls that alert members of a group to potential threats, to softer cooing noises that seem to be used in a more intimate context. Recent studies have even pointed to the possibility that crows have the ability to learn new sounds and potentially even mimic human speech, although this area is still subject to ongoing research.

Emotional Intelligence

While the study of emotions in animals is a complex and controversial field, there are some indications that corvids may possess what can be termed as emotional intelligence. Observations have been made of crows participating in what appears to be "funerals"—a ritualistic gathering around a deceased member, which has been interpreted by some researchers as a way of processing grief or learning about dangers that led to the death.

Neurological Basis for Intelligence

All these complex behaviors and cognitive skills have a neurological basis. The crow brain, despite its small size relative to body mass, has a high degree of encephalization—the ratio of brain mass to body mass—that is comparable to some primates. Specifically, the regions associated with problem-solving and complex thinking are highly developed.

Harmonizing Science with the Mystical

While the empirical data on corvids can sometimes seem to clash with their mystical representation, a balanced view would suggest that one realm can enrich the other. Understanding the scientific facets of corvid intelligence makes their roles in mythology and folklore even more fascinating. One could argue that our ancestors, in their own way, were recognizing the same intelligence and social complexity in crows that science is now confirming.

In sum, modern science provides an array of tools that deepen our understanding of corvid intelligence and cognition. Whether it's their impressive problem-solving skills, social behaviors, or complex communication, research continually reveals the remarkable capabilities of these birds. As we venture further into the mystical realms in later chapters, let this scientific perspective serve as a grounding element, showing us that there are multiple ways to appreciate and connect with the magnificent world of corvids.

1.3 STRUCTURE
OF THE BOOK

In the journey you are about to undertake, understanding the roadmap can be as enlightening as the voyage itself. This book, "Meditations with Crows: Messages from the Corvid Realm," aims to be your comprehensive guide through the complex and enchanting universe of corvids. This chapter aims to shed light on how the book is structured and how each section will help you deepen your connection with the mystical and scientific world of crows and their kin.

The Balanced Approach

A harmonious balance between the scientific and mystical realms forms the cornerstone of this book. While the enigma surrounding corvids has been steeped in myth and spirituality, recent years have seen burgeoning scientific interest in their intelligence, behavior, and ecological roles. The book is meticulously designed to honor both perspectives, offering a rounded understanding that respects tradition while embracing modern discoveries.

Navigating Chapters

The book is divided into twelve key chapters, each one exploring different facets of human-corvid interactions, spiritual practices, and scientific perspectives.

Chapters 1-3 lay the foundation by introducing you to the world of corvids from both mystical and scientific viewpoints. From ancient myths to cutting-edge research, these chapters aim to build your background knowledge.

Chapters 4-7 dive deeper into the practices that allow a more intimate connection with the corvid realm. This includes exploring the concept of synchronicities, detailing meditation techniques, and even venturing into more advanced spiritual practices like shamanic journeying and astral projection.

Chapters 8-10 focus on the practical applications of your newfound knowledge and spiritual practices. You'll discover how the wisdom of crows can enrich your daily life, relationships, and even your professional journey.

Chapter 11 serves as a guide to further resources for those who wish to delve even deeper, offering recommendations on literature, online communities, and courses that can augment your understanding and practice.

Finally, Chapter 12 will offer concluding thoughts and reflect on future prospects in the expanding field of human-corvid relationships, leaving you with a profound message to carry forward.

Real-Life Narratives and Case Studies

One of the unique features of this book is the integration of real-life accounts and scientific case studies. These are not just abstract concepts but lived experiences and researched phenomena. You'll read testimonies of people who have successfully meditated with crows, backed by scientific studies that resonate with these personal narratives.

Expert Insights

To provide a multi-dimensional view, insights from experts in various fields—be it spirituality, ecology, or animal behavior—will be interspersed throughout the book. Their perspectives will enrich your understanding and perhaps inspire you to explore the topic from multiple angles.

A Resource for Further Exploration

Beyond its immediate contents, the book aims to be a springboard for your own exploration. An extensive resource section will guide you to further avenues of study and community involvement, should you wish to extend your journey beyond these pages.

In summary, this book aims to be a tapestry of knowledge, experiences, and practical tools that will guide you through the enthralling world of corvids. Whether you are scientifically inclined, spiritually interested, or simply curious, there's something in this book for you. By its end, you should have a well-rounded understanding of corvids that bridges scientific inquiry and spiritual connection, enriching not just your knowledge but potentially, the quality of your life.

CHAPTER 2:
UNDERSTANDING
CORVID BEHAVIOR

2.1 SOCIAL STRUCTURE

Corvids, the family of birds that includes crows, ravens, magpies, and jays, are not just ordinary birds that one might encounter in a backyard or on a nature trail. They are exceptionally social creatures with intricate community dynamics. These social structures are complex and adaptive, exhibiting traits like cooperation, altruism, and even deception. Understanding the social fabric of corvid communities can offer not just scientific insights but also spiritual meanings, and can deepen our appreciation for these highly intelligent beings.

Familial Bonds

Family is at the core of a corvid's life. They often live in family groups and engage in communal caregiving. In many species, the young stay with their parents for an extended period, sometimes even up to two years, to learn the various skills and social dynamics necessary for survival. There's a reciprocal nature to these familial relationships. Older siblings often assist in raising the younger ones, a trait known as "cooperative breeding." This not only benefits the family unit but also provides invaluable learning experiences for the younger birds.

Hierarchies and Dominance

Corvids establish social hierarchies within their groups, and these hierarchies influence the access to resources, mates, and nesting sites. Dominant birds are often more experienced and older, taking on a sort of "elder" role in the community. However, hierarchies are not static. Younger or lower-ranking birds can ascend the social ladder through a combination of intelligence, cunning, and social maneuvering. Studies show that crows can recognize the dominant and subordinate members within their own groups and even in other groups, which indicates a nuanced understanding of power dynamics.

Social Learning and Culture

One of the most fascinating aspects of corvid social structure is the element of culture and social learning. Just as humans pass down traditions and knowledge, so do these birds. For example, New Caledonian crows are famous for their tool-making abilities, a skill that is taught from generation to generation. Furthermore, different crow communities have been observed employing unique problem-solving techniques and even dialects in their calls, akin to localized "languages." This points to the existence of a corvid "culture," built upon generational knowledge and adapted to local circumstances.

Altruism and Cooperation

Corvids have been observed engaging in behaviors that suggest a level of altruism and cooperation rarely seen in the animal kingdom. For example, food sharing is common among them, even when the act doesn't offer immediate, tangible benefits. In some instances, crows have been known to give gifts to humans who feed them, further mystifying our understanding of their social dynamics. Cooperation extends to problem-solving as well; for example, a group of crows will often work together to gain access to food sources or to fend off predators. Such behaviors indicate not just cognitive sophistication but also emotional complexity, providing a rich tapestry for both scientific and spiritual exploration.

Conflict and Deception

Like any society, conflicts do arise within corvid communities. These birds have been observed employing a variety of tactics to deceive each other, especially when it comes to food storage. Crows, for instance, have been observed pretending to hide food, leading other crows astray, and then hiding the food in a different location when unobserved. This shows that they not only recognize the intentions of others but can actively manipulate those perceptions for their own benefit. While this might appear as a "darker" aspect of their social nature, it also reveals their ability to strategize and think several steps ahead.

In summary, the social structures within corvid communities are far from simple. They display a range of complex behaviors, from familial bonds and hierarchical structures to altruism and even deception. These behaviors are not just survival tactics but are deeply ingrained in the corvid way of life, providing a window into their emotional and cognitive worlds. As we explore these dimensions, we can gain insights not just for scientific understanding but for a richer, more holistic appreciation of these truly remarkable beings.

2.2 COMMUNICATION SKILLS

Corvids are not just social marvels; they are also prodigious communicators. To understand the depth and complexity of their communication, one must delve into the myriad ways they interact through vocalizations, body language, and even the use of tools. Communication in the corvid realm serves multiple purposes: conveying information about food, warning of predators, and maintaining social bonds, to name a few.

Vocalizations

Corvid vocalizations are a topic of keen interest among researchers and bird enthusiasts alike. Crows, for instance, have been observed to have different types of calls: alarm calls, feeding calls, and calls that are used to rally others. Some studies even suggest that they may possess regional "dialects," further highlighting the intricacy of their vocal communication system. In ravens, research conducted by ethologists indicates that their vocal repertoire is among the most complex in the avian world, consisting of various types of calls that can signal everything from playfulness to distress.

These calls are not arbitrary noises; they convey important information that helps corvids survive and thrive in their environment. Alarm calls, for example, are immediate and loud, alerting members of the group to potential threats. Conversely, feeding calls are generally softer and used to gather others for a shared meal, underscoring the role of vocalizations in fostering community bonds.

Body Language

Aside from their vocal expressions, corvids also employ a sophisticated system of body language. Postures, movements, and even feather displays play a critical role in how they interact with one another. Dominant crows, for example, often puff up their feathers and hold their wings out slightly to establish their status, while submissive individuals might crouch and lower their heads. During courtship, male crows frequently perform aerial acrobatics, such as swoops and dives, to impress potential mates. Ravens, on the other hand, use gentle beak touching and mutual preening to reinforce their bonds.

The body language of corvids can be quite nuanced and situation-dependent. For instance, a raised wing or tail feather may have different implications depending on the context in which it is displayed. This level of complexity suggests that corvid body language goes beyond mere instinctual responses and may involve a certain degree of intentionality.

Tools for Communication

While the use of tools is generally associated with problem-solving, there are instances where corvids have used tools to communicate. In one study, captive crows were observed using sticks to get the attention of humans when they wanted access to food or water. This behavior demonstrates that corvids are capable of using external objects not just to manipulate their environment but also to convey messages to other species.

The Importance of Listening

For humans interested in meditating or connecting with the corvid realm, understanding the subtleties of their communication is crucial. The calls and body language of these birds can provide insights into their emotional states, intentions, and even their social dynamics. By paying close attention to these signals, one may deepen their understanding and appreciation of these remarkable birds, paving the way for a more meaningful interaction and spiritual connection.

In summary, the communication skills of corvids are remarkably complex and serve various purposes, including the transmission of crucial survival information and the maintenance of social bonds. Their sophisticated vocalizations, nuanced body language, and innovative use of tools for communication make them one of the most intelligent and expressive avian species. For anyone looking to connect with the corvid realm, whether through meditation or simple observation, a deep understanding of their communication methods can only enrich the experience.

2.3 PROBLEM-SOLVING AND ADAPTABILITY

Just as you may adapt and innovate when faced with obstacles in your life, corvids demonstrate remarkable skills in problem-solving and adaptability. The ability to adjust to varying environmental conditions and solve complex problems is often considered a hallmark of intelligence, and in this regard, corvids stand out as avian geniuses.

The Toolbox of Corvids

Perhaps one of the most astonishing facets of corvid intelligence is their use of tools. New Caledonian crows, for instance, have been observed using twigs, leaves, and even their feathers to extract insects from tree bark. What's more, these crows not only use tools but also modify them according to the task at hand, showcasing their ability for advanced problem-solving. This kind of behavior has long been thought to be a unique attribute of primates, but the corvid family challenges this notion.

The tools aren't just used for foraging. Corvids have been seen using cars to crack open nuts by placing them on roadways and waiting for vehicles to run over them. This not only highlights their problem-solving abilities but also their incredible adaptability to the human-made environment.

Cognitive Flexibility

The adaptability of corvids extends well beyond their toolbox. Research has shown that these birds possess what's called "cognitive flexibility," which allows them to alter their behavior in response to changing circumstances. This trait is particularly important in social interactions, where the ability to interpret and react to the actions of other birds can be critical for survival.

For example, certain studies have indicated that some corvids are capable of tactical deception—a rare phenomenon in the animal kingdom. Eurasian jays, for instance, have been observed hiding food caches while looking over their shoulders, as if aware they are being watched and possibly learning from experience when their caches are raided by others. This not only demonstrates problem-solving but also suggests a level of social awareness and understanding of other individuals' perspectives, a trait often ascribed to humans and some primates.

Adaptation to Urban Environments

The increasing human encroachment into natural habitats makes adaptability an essential skill for wildlife. Corvids have shown a striking ability to thrive in urban settings, where they find novel ways to make use of available resources. For example, in addition to their nut-cracking strategy, they have been known to pick through trash to find food, nest in man-made structures, and even steal from human food supplies.

Interestingly, their adaptability is not just limited to physical actions but extends to their cognitive functions. Studies have shown that urban crows are more adept at problem-solving tasks compared to their rural counterparts, suggesting that complex environments like cities might actually stimulate cognitive development.

The Intricacies of Corvid Play

Beyond their daily needs for survival, corvids also indulge in play, another sign of their advanced cognitive capabilities. This form of engagement with their environment and peers allows them to practice essential skills and understand the physics of the world around them. Whether it's crows snowboarding down rooftops on cardboard pieces or young ravens teasing and playing games with each other, these activities likely serve both as cognitive stimulation and social bonding.

Play often involves complex aerobatics, object manipulation, and even games that appear to have rules understood among the playing birds. It's not merely aimless or frivolous activity; it's an essential aspect of their complex social lives and another example of their problem-solving skills. In this sense, play is an evolutionary advantage that enhances adaptability.

In summary, the realm of corvid behavior offers us a fascinating window into the cognitive flexibility, problem-solving skills, and adaptability of these birds. From employing and modifying tools to adapting to urban environments and engaging in complex social interactions, corvids are more than just black-feathered birds with a caw; they're an embodiment of avian intelligence and adaptability. Whether you're an enthusiast looking to deepen your connection through meditation or a researcher exploring the boundaries of animal cognition, understanding the intellectual capabilities of corvids can offer enriching insights into not just their world, but also our own.

CHAPTER 3:
SYMBOLISM AND
MYTHOLOGY

3.1 CULTURAL SYMBOLISM

In the vast tapestry of human history and beliefs, crows have consistently flown into our myths, stories, and daily lives, carrying with them a train of symbolism rich in nuance and diversity. Whether portrayed as messengers of the gods or emblems of transformation, the symbolism linked with these intelligent birds differs from culture to culture, capturing a wide range of human experiences and perspectives.

Eastern Traditions

In Asian cultures, crows hold various symbolic meanings. In Hindu mythology, crows are considered to be messengers and servants of Lord Shani, the god of justice. They are believed to convey the prayers of humans to the heavens and bring back divine messages. In Japan, the crow or "karasu" is deeply embedded in folklore and religion. They are considered guardians and protectors, often linked with the Shinto deity, Amaterasu, the goddess of the Sun. Similarly, in Chinese tradition, crows are often seen as a symbol of filial piety because of their observed behavior of caring for their elderly and sick.

Native American Perspectives

Among the Native American tribes, crows are regarded with a mix of reverence and wariness. In some stories, they are clever tricksters who can change the course of rivers and steal fire for humanity, much like Prometheus in Greek mythology. In others, they are omens of change or carriers of spiritual messages. Different tribes have distinct perspectives; for instance, the Crow tribe of Montana highly respects the crow and sees it as a symbol of sacred law.

European Views

In Europe, the crow's symbolism is more dualistic. In Celtic mythology, the crow is associated with the Morrigan, the goddess of war and fate. Crows in this context are often seen as harbingers of doom but also as symbols of transformation and rebirth. In Norse mythology, Odin, the Allfather, is often pictured with two crows, Huginn (thought) and Muninn (memory), who fly all over the world to bring news to him. Here, crows are seen as highly intelligent, wise, and deeply connected to the divine.

African Narratives

In African cultures, crows often appear in folklore as wise creatures that outwit larger, stronger animals. They symbolize intelligence and resourcefulness. In some regions, crows are also considered as intermediaries between the living and the ancestral spirits, serving a similar role to that in Eastern and Native American beliefs.

Modern Interpretations

In the contemporary Western world, crows often get a bad rap as omens of bad luck or as nuisances. However, there is a growing movement to reinterpret and reclaim their symbolism, drawing from both ancient traditions and modern observations of their remarkable intelligence and social complexity. They are increasingly being viewed as symbols of adaptability and resourcefulness, especially in urban environments where they have thrived.

Understanding the wide array of symbolism attached to crows across various cultures allows us to appreciate not just the bird itself but also the human experience that it reflects. Our stories and myths, after all, say as much about us as they do about the creatures they feature. In learning about how different cultures view crows, we open ourselves to a richer, more nuanced understanding of this remarkable bird, and by extension, the world we share with it.

3.2 MYTHOLOGICAL SIGNIFICANCE

Myths and legends often serve as rich tapestries where the natural world meets human imagination. Crows and other corvids are no strangers to these storytelling realms. Throughout history, in different corners of the world, these fascinating birds have been characters in tales that explore the essence of life, death, and the complexities of existence.

Ancient Myths

Greek mythology offers one of the most well-known roles for the crow. In one story, Apollo, the god of light, music, and prophecy, sent a crow to fetch a cup of water. The crow returned late, carrying a water snake as an excuse for his tardiness. Angered, Apollo turned the crow's feathers from white to black. In another tale, the crow serves Athena, the goddess of wisdom, as a messenger. These stories not only highlight the perceived intelligence of the crow but also emphasize its ability to interact with deities, showcasing the bird's higher symbolic value.

In Hindu mythology, crows are considered to be ancestors, and there is a specific day called "Kakbhushundi," dedicated to honoring them. During this time, food offerings are made to crows as it's believed they carry souls to the afterlife. Here, the crow serves as a symbol of transition and a mediator between worlds.

Celtic and Norse Mythologies

In Celtic mythology, the crow is often associated with the Morrígan, a figure who embodies fate, war, and death. The crow, in this case, becomes a symbol of both the prophetic and the ominous. Crows are also thought to possess the power to move between worlds, acting as messengers between the earthly realm and the otherworld.

Norse mythology also honors the crow—or rather, two ravens named Huginn (thought) and Muninn (memory)—as constant companions to Odin, the Allfather. Every day, these ravens would fly out to gather news and whisper it into Odin's ears. This dual presence of thought and memory gives a complex dimension to corvid symbolism, emphasizing their association with wisdom and knowledge.

Native American Tales

In many Native American cultures, the crow holds a special place as a trickster figure. In some tribes like the Tlingit and the Haida, the crow is considered a cultural hero who steals the sun to bring light to the world. Though often cunning and deceitful, the crow's actions bring about necessary change and transformation. This duality aligns with the broader complexity of the crow's symbolic significance.

East Asian Lore

In Chinese folklore, the crow is a positive symbol representing the sun, based on the ancient belief that crows were capable of carrying the sun in their beaks. In Japanese mythology, a three-legged crow called Yatagarasu serves as a guide and an imperial symbol, thought to represent divine intervention in human affairs.

African Folktales

In African myths, the crow often appears as both wise and foolish, encapsulating the paradoxes of life. In these stories, crows are sometimes seen as symbols of resourcefulness and cleverness but also as figures that caution against the perils of overconfidence.

In summary, whether they are messengers to the gods, carriers of the sun, or trickster heroes, crows and their corvid cousins have found their way into myths and legends across cultures. These roles don't merely add intriguing narratives; they offer layers of understanding to the bird's natural behaviors and characteristics. This rich mythological tapestry further enhances the corvid's place in our collective consciousness, offering a multifaceted lens through which to explore and meditate upon these captivating creatures.

3.3 CONTEMPORARY USE

The presence of crows in the mythologies and cultures of the past is undeniable, but what about the modern era? Crows and other corvids continue to captivate our imagination, marking their presence felt in literature, art, and even popular media. This chapter aims to explore how the symbolism of crows permeates various facets of contemporary expression.

Literature and Poetry

The crow, often symbolizing intelligence, transformation, and sometimes foreboding, has not lost its allure in modern literary works. Numerous contemporary authors, from mystery to fantasy genres, often utilize the crow or raven as a symbol or even as a character. For example, in Haruki Murakami's "Kafka on the Shore," the enigmatic figure of Johnny Walker has a menacing crow companion, a representation of the surreal and mysterious elements in the story. Similarly, the crow appears in various works of poetry, often serving as a metaphor for change, self-reflection, or even political critique.

Visual Arts

In the world of art, the crow has been a recurring motif across various media. Whether it's a painting, sculpture, or even a digital art piece, artists often employ the image of a crow to evoke specific emotions or messages. The stark black plumage of the crow can create a dramatic contrast in visual compositions, while its intelligent gaze adds an element of intrigue. Even in street art and graffiti, the crow serves as an adaptable symbol for a range of issues from societal decay to hope and resilience.

Music and Film

The crow's influence is not confined to static media. In music, they have been the subject or inspiration for songs across genres. A band like The Black Crowes openly embraces the symbolism, and individual songs often reference the bird as a symbol of freedom or even impending doom. In films, crows have been portrayed as omens, spies, and messengers. Films like "The Crow" (1994) use the bird as a central piece of its narrative, underlining themes of death and rebirth. Likewise, animated features like Hayao Miyazaki's "Spirited Away" include crows as characters that embody wisdom and guidance.

Branding and Commercial Use

In a rather unexpected turn, the crow has also found its way into the realm of branding and advertising. Given the bird's association with intelligence and adaptability, tech companies and educational platforms sometimes incorporate crow imagery into their logos or marketing materials. Even some sports teams, like the Adelaide Crows in the Australian Football League, choose the crow as their mascot to symbolize teamwork and cunning strategy.

Social and Political Narratives

Finally, in an era characterized by rapid social and technological changes, the crow serves as an adaptable symbol in social justice movements and political narratives. For instance, environmental campaigns may use the image of a crow or raven to symbolize the wisdom of living sustainably and respecting natural ecosystems. In political cartoons, the crow can represent various elements, from cunning politicians to insightful social critiques, reflecting the multifaceted symbolism carried from historical contexts into present-day interpretations.

In summary, the crow's symbolism is not stuck in the annals of history but is a dynamic and evolving aspect of contemporary culture. Whether it's through literature, art, music, branding, or even social narratives, the crow remains a potent symbol, adaptable and relevant to the challenges and themes of modern life. Thus, the captivating aura that has historically surrounded these intelligent birds continues to thrive in myriad ways, confirming that our fascination with crows is far from over.

CHAPTER 4:
MESSAGES AND SYNCHRONICITIES

4.1 UNDERSTANDING SYNCHRONICITIES

The idea of synchronicity tends to evoke a sense of wonder, akin to the feeling you get when a seemingly random event offers surprising meaning or personal insight. Swiss psychiatrist Carl Jung first introduced the concept of synchronicity as a "meaningful coincidence," where external events resonate with internal states, seemingly without a cause-and-effect relationship. In the context of our exploration of crows and the corvid realm, the concept of synchronicity takes on a particularly mystical nuance. In this chapter, we'll delve into the notion of synchronicities as they relate to interactions with crows, examining how these events might not be coincidental at all but deeply connected to personal and collective subconscious.

The Basics of Synchronicity

Synchronicity is often experienced as a meaningful coincidence where two or more events, which might not have any apparent causal relationship, happen in such a way that their occurrence together has special significance. For instance, you might be pondering a significant life decision and suddenly, a crow appears before you, cawing loudly as if urging you to make your choice. Though science would categorize this as a mere coincidence, from the standpoint of synchronicity, the crow's appearance might be seen as a meaningful event in relation to your internal dilemma.

Synchronicity and Collective Unconscious

Carl Jung posited that synchronicities tap into what he called the "collective unconscious," a shared reservoir of symbols, archetypes, and experiences that transcend individual psyches. The concept of the collective unconscious offers a theoretical basis for understanding how crows, which hold symbolic weight in various cultures as messengers or omens, could be part of such synchronistic events. According to Jungian psychology, crows, laden with universal symbolism, may act as agents that help to surface latent content from our collective unconscious, providing meaningful interactions that resonate with our inner states.

The Role of Intuition and Perception

To engage with synchronicity requires a certain attunement to one's intuition and perception. It's not so much about interpreting the crow's behavior or appearance through a strict logical lens as it is about feeling into the moment and perceiving connections that might not be immediately apparent. Essentially, your awareness and openness determine your ability to pick up on these synchronistic events. The intuitive nature of recognizing synchronicities can make it a subjective experience, which often complicates scientific validation.

Scientific Skepticism and Openness

Science often regards events classified as synchronicities as coincidences because they can't be explained by conventional cause-and-effect logic. While it's crucial to approach such phenomena with a healthy degree of skepticism, an overly rigid viewpoint might close off avenues for understanding the deeper layers of human experience. Some scholars, like physicist David Bohm, have suggested that synchronicities could be linked to the "implicate order," a term he used to describe an underlying order in the universe where everything is interconnected. This idea, although speculative, opens up possibilities for reconciling scientific and mystical perspectives on synchronicity.

Synchronicity and Spiritual Practices

Many spiritual traditions and practices, including shamanism and certain forms of meditation, place a high value on meaningful coincidences and regard them as messages or guidance from the spiritual realm. In the case of interactions with crows, these synchronicities might be considered messages from the corvid realm—a way the universe communicates its wisdom through these intelligent birds. Through mindful observation and meditative practices, one can develop a heightened sensitivity to such events, seeing them not as random occurrences but as signposts on a spiritual journey.

In summary, the concept of synchronicity provides a framework for understanding the meaningful coincidences that often occur when interacting with crows. While skepticism exists, primarily from scientific quarters, the richness of personal experience and the potential for spiritual growth through these synchronistic events should not be dismissed. Recognizing and engaging with synchronicities may offer deeply personal insights and serve as transformative experiences, further deepening our connection with the intriguing and ever-mysterious corvid realm.

4.2 READING SIGNS

Observing crows in the natural world or even in the heart of a bustling city can provide illuminating insights, but knowing how to interpret these insights is essential for a deeper understanding of their messages. Whether it's the way a crow looks at you, the patterns of their flight, or their specific calls, each behavior can be considered a form of communication. The following techniques and approaches can help you read the signs conveyed by the presence or behavior of crows.

Crow Behavior and Context

The first step to reading signs from crows is to pay attention to their behavior in context. For example, a crow cawing on a tree branch may not have the same meaning as one that drops a shiny object in front of you. Context is key; observe what the crow is doing, where it is doing it, and when it is happening.

Additionally, consider the environmental conditions: time of day, weather, and even the season. For example, crows are known to be more active during certain weather patterns and less so during others. Observing these nuances can help you form a more nuanced understanding of their messages.

Numerology and Patterns

Numbers often play an important role in spiritual symbolism, and the same can be said for crows. Multiple crows can signify different things depending on their number. For instance, a common lore suggests that one crow signifies sorrow, two crows signify joy, three indicate a wedding, and so on. However, always be cautious of following such norms rigidly. Personal meanings can often override traditional beliefs, and it's essential to combine both for a comprehensive understanding.

Patterns, like the repetition of certain behaviors or events, can also provide valuable insights. For example, if you repeatedly encounter crows during significant life events or transitions, this could be a sign that you should be more attentive to changes or decisions in your life.

Body Language and Vocalization

Crows have a varied range of calls and body movements that serve specific purposes. For example, a caw could be a simple call to alert the community, or it could be a specific message to you. Learning to distinguish between different types of caws or paying attention to other vocalizations can be crucial for interpreting their messages. Body language, such as the direction a crow faces, the spread of its wings, or even the tilt of its head, can offer additional layers of meaning.

Synchronicity and Personal Relevance

It's crucial to align crow observations with personal life events or questions you might be contemplating. In the realm of synchronicities, seemingly random encounters with crows can often relate to current issues or questions you might have. Keep a journal to note down these experiences, and over time, patterns may emerge that link crow behaviors to specific events or feelings in your life.

Trust Your Intuition

Finally, trust your gut feelings when interpreting signs and symbols from crows. Intuition is the sum total of your life experiences, and it can often guide you accurately in decoding messages that are personally relevant. Your internal compass can provide a vital layer of interpretation that intellectual analysis might miss.

In summary, reading signs from crows involves a careful mix of observation, context understanding, and intuitive insight. By paying attention to their behavior, accounting for the context and environmental factors, noticing numbers and patterns, understanding their body language and vocalization, and finally, trusting your own intuition, you can deepen your connection to the corvid realm and uncover the wealth of wisdom it has to offer.

4.3 PERSONAL EXPERIENCES

Anecdotes and personal testimonies often serve as rich, qualitative data that breathe life into theories and abstract concepts. In the realm of corvid interactions, stories from individuals who have had profound experiences with these intelligent birds offer unique insights. Such accounts illuminate the subtle ways in which the world of crows intersects with human consciousness, often in the form of messages and synchronicities. Below are a few curated experiences that may resonate with you and provide tangible examples of how meditating with crows can manifest into powerful life experiences.

Crow as a Compass

One remarkable account comes from a woman named Jane who found herself at a crossroads in life, questioning her career path. She recalls walking in a local park, engrossed in thought, when a crow perched on a nearby bench caught her attention. Intrigued, she took a moment to sit and quietly observe the bird. She noted that the crow seemed to be tilting its head as if to inspect something on the ground. Following its gaze, Jane discovered a tarnished old compass partially buried in the dirt. Taking it as a sign, she decided to redirect her career path, and soon thereafter, landed a job that was more aligned with her passions. Whether coincidence or synchronicity, the compass and the crow were instrumental in guiding her toward a life-changing decision.

A Resounding Call

Tim, an avid birdwatcher, recounts a poignant moment when a crow's call seemed to echo his inner turmoil. During a period of grief after the loss of a close family member, Tim heard a crow's distinctive caw while visiting the cemetery. The sound was so arresting that it snapped him out of his thoughts and grounded him in the moment. He felt as though the crow was sharing in his sorrow, its calls reflecting the deep emotional state he was going through. Although it didn't eliminate his pain, the crow's presence offered him a form of subtle comfort and understanding, a shared companionship in a difficult moment.

Gift of Gratitude

Another compelling experience involves a man named Alex, who had been feeding a family of crows in his backyard for several months. Over time, Alex began to find small trinkets near the food tray—shiny pieces of metal, buttons, and even a key. These 'gifts' were known behavioral traits of crows, who are observed to bring presents as tokens of appreciation. For Alex, these gifts became symbols of a deeper connection with the corvid family, an acknowledgment of a shared relationship that went beyond just the feeding.

Visionary Dreams

Finally, a woman named Emily, deeply involved in spiritual practices, had recurring dreams featuring a crow. In her dreams, the crow would guide her through various landscapes, leading her to doors she hadn't noticed in her waking life. When she decided to meditate on these dreams, she experienced visions that offered solutions to personal challenges she had been facing. The crow, serving as a spiritual guide in her dream state, symbolized her unconscious wisdom steering her towards answers she was seeking.

These accounts, each unique in its context and depth, share a common thread of meaningful interaction with crows. Whether it's through physical signs, emotional resonance, reciprocal relationships, or dreams, these stories demonstrate that the presence and actions of crows can be interpreted as synchronicities or messages that have personal significance.

In sum, personal experiences with crows add a layer of richness and intricacy to our understanding of these enigmatic birds. Whether viewed as mere coincidence or meaningful synchronicity is a matter of personal belief. What remains clear is that these accounts open up possibilities for deeper human-corvid relationships, inviting us to explore further and to attune ourselves to the messages that may be waiting for us in the winged whispers of the crow.

CHAPTER 5:
PREPARING FOR
MEDITATION

5.1 CREATING SACRED SPACE

Creating a sacred space is an integral step in preparing for meaningful meditation, particularly when seeking to connect with the remarkable and mystical corvid realm. This space serves as a physical and emotional sanctuary where you can feel relaxed, focused, and attuned to the energies you wish to explore. In this chapter, we will guide you through the essentials of setting up such a space that fosters a deep connection with the corvid realm.

Choosing the Right Location

The location for your sacred space plays a vital role in the effectiveness of your meditation. Ideally, choose a spot that is quiet and free from disturbances. The importance of silence, or at least minimized background noise, cannot be overstated. Noise pollution can be a significant distraction and make it challenging to dive deep into meditative states. If an outdoor space is available to you, consider setting up your sacred space in nature. The natural elements often enhance spiritual connectivity, and being in the outdoors offers the added benefit of a possible encounter with crows or other corvids.

The Significance of Orientation

In various spiritual traditions, the cardinal directions—North, South, East, and West—hold unique meanings and energies. North may symbolize groundedness and stability, while East might represent new beginnings. When setting up your space, you may choose to align it with a particular direction that resonates with your intentions. You can use a simple compass or a smartphone app to determine the directions. Incorporating these beliefs can add a layer of spiritual depth to your meditative practices.

Elemental Considerations

In many spiritual paths, the classical elements—Earth, Water, Air, and Fire—are important. These elements can be subtly or explicitly included in your sacred space to facilitate a well-rounded energetic experience.

Earth: Consider adding plants, crystals, or a bowl of soil to connect with the grounding energy of the Earth.

Water: A small bowl of water or a water feature can be included to encourage emotional fluidity and intuitive insights.

Air: Incense, bells, or feathers (perhaps a crow feather if you come across one naturally) can represent the element of air, aiding in intellectual clarity and spiritual communication.

Fire: A candle or an oil lamp can represent the fire element, invoking transformation and inner illumination.

Personal Artifacts and Symbolism

Items that hold personal or spiritual significance can also be placed in your sacred space. This could be anything from family heirlooms to spiritual texts. Given the focus on corvids, you might include artwork or statues of crows or ravens. Personal artifacts serve as anchors for your intentions and make the space distinctly yours.

Energetic Cleansing

Before using the space for meditation, it's a good idea to cleanse it energetically. This can be done through various means like smudging with sage, using salt water, or even through sound vibrations using bells or singing bowls. The idea is to clear the space of any lingering energies so that it is a neutral platform where new energies can be invoked and cultivated.

Accessibility and Practicality

While the aesthetics and energetic components of the space are important, it's equally crucial for the space to be accessible and practical. It should be a place where you can sit comfortably for extended periods. If you choose an outdoor space, ensure that it is safe and offers some level of privacy. If you're setting up indoors, make sure you won't be easily distracted by household or work-related tasks. Your sacred space should invite you to step away from the mundane and into the mystical.

In summary, creating a sacred space involves more than just designating a spot for meditation; it's about creating an environment that aligns with your intentions and spiritual inclinations. Through the thoughtful inclusion of various elements, directions, and personal artifacts, you construct a sanctuary that enriches your quest for a deeper connection with the corvid realm. This preparation sets the stage for you to explore the breathing techniques and intentions that will be discussed in subsequent chapters, further equipping you for a rewarding journey into the mysterious and enlightening world of corvids.

5.2 BREATHING TECHNIQUES

Breathing is a natural, involuntary process that we often take for granted. However, when it comes to meditation and particularly the pursuit of connecting with the corvid realm, breathwork takes on an even more critical role. Proper breathing techniques can serve as a bridge between your physical self and the mystical energies surrounding crows and other corvids. These methods help center your thoughts, bring attention to the present moment, and prepare your consciousness for the more advanced practices described in later chapters.

The Physiology of Breath

Before diving into the breathing exercises, let's take a moment to appreciate the physiological aspects of breathing. When you breathe, oxygen fills your lungs and is then transferred to your bloodstream, which circulates this essential element throughout your body. Carbon dioxide, a waste product, is expelled during exhalation. This basic yet intricate process plays a crucial role in maintaining your body's pH balance, regulating temperature, and supporting cellular functions. Mindful breathing, an act of consciously controlling your breath, can also significantly impact your nervous system, reducing stress hormones and facilitating relaxation.

Diaphragmatic Breathing

Diaphragmatic breathing, commonly referred to as "belly breathing," is a simple yet effective technique that emphasizes full oxygen exchange. Unlike shallow chest breathing, this method ensures that you use the diaphragm, a large muscle at the base of the lungs, rather than relying on the smaller muscles located in your upper chest. Practicing this can lead to a more relaxed state, providing a beneficial foundation for your meditative pursuits.

To perform diaphragmatic breathing:

- Sit or lie down in a comfortable position.
- Place one hand on your chest and the other on your abdomen.
- Inhale deeply through your nose, allowing your abdomen to expand fully, while keeping the chest relatively still.
- Exhale completely through your mouth, noting the movement of your abdomen and the minimal movement of your chest.

Repeat for several cycles, aiming to extend the length of each inhalation and exhalation gradually.

4-7-8 Technique

The 4-7-8 breathing technique, inspired by ancient yogic practices, can be particularly effective in calming the mind and preparing it for a deeper meditative state.

To practice this technique:

- Inhale quietly through the nose for a count of 4.
- Hold the breath for a count of 7.

- Exhale completely through the mouth for a count of 8.

Complete this cycle for four breaths initially, and gradually work your way up to eight cycles.

Breath Awareness

Sometimes, the best way to connect with the breath is simply to observe it without trying to modify it in any way. This practice, known as breath awareness, fosters a sense of present-moment consciousness, facilitating a deeper meditative state. Simply shutting your eyes and paying great attention to the rhythm of your natural breathing is all that is required of you. Become aware of the air passing through your nose, the rising and falling of your abdomen, and the slowing down of both your body and your mind as a result of this.

Integrating Breathwork into Your Meditative Routine

Breathwork doesn't have to be an isolated practice; you can seamlessly incorporate these techniques into your broader meditative routine. For instance, you can commence with a few minutes of diaphragmatic breathing to settle into your meditation session. Follow this with the 4-7-8 technique to delve deeper into relaxation, and finally, shift into breath awareness as you transition into more advanced meditation practices focused on connecting with the corvid realm.

In summary, understanding and practicing effective breathing techniques are instrumental in preparing both your body and mind for deeper meditation and connection with the corvid realm. Whether you are a beginner or an experienced practitioner, breathwork can provide a supportive foundation upon which you can build your spiritual endeavors, enhancing not only your meditative experiences but also your overall well-being.

5.3 SETTING INTENTIONS

Embarking on a meditative journey requires more than just a quiet space and a settled mind. One of the fundamental elements that can greatly impact the quality and outcome of your meditation is the intention you set before you begin. Intention setting is a practice that aligns your mental, emotional, and spiritual energies toward a specific goal or inquiry. In the context of meditations with crows, setting a clear and focused intention can serve as a bridge that connects you to the wisdom and guidance that the corvid realm has to offer.

The Importance of Intention

An intention is often likened to a compass that guides you through the meditative landscape. It acts as an anchor, providing you with a direction to follow, or a question to explore. Unlike a goal, which is a specific outcome you desire, an intention is more of an open-ended yet focused inquiry. It aligns your energies and thoughts in a particular direction but leaves room for surprise and discovery. According to research in the field of psychology, setting an intention can have a potent effect on cognitive functions, including attention and memory, thereby enhancing the overall meditative experience.

Tips for Setting an Effective Intention

The process of setting an intention can be both simple and profound. Here are some tips to guide you:

Be Specific Yet Open: While your intention should be specific, it should not be restrictive. For example, an intention like "I want to understand the corvid realm" is specific but allows room for various forms of understanding to manifest.

Use Positive Language: The language you use to set your intention matters. Instead of framing it in the negative, such as "I don't want to be afraid," try using positive language like "I seek courage."

Tap into Your Emotions: The process of defining intentions involves not only mental but also emotional labor. What are you interested in exploring? A layer of authenticity can be added to by tapping into the feelings that you are experiencing.

Write it Down: There's something powerful about putting your intention into written form. It serves as a tangible reminder of what you're seeking and can be referred to during your meditation for added focus.

Speak It Aloud: If it resonates with you, saying your intention aloud can further solidify it and bring it into the realm of manifestation.

Integrating Intentions in Corvid Meditations

When meditating with the aim of connecting with crows or the corvid realm, your intention could vary widely depending on what you're drawn to. You may wish to understand the wisdom crows hold, explore their symbolism in your life, or simply develop a deeper connection with them. Your intention will act as an energetic invitation, allowing you to tune into the frequencies of the corvid realm.

Before starting your meditation, you might visualize a crow or imagine the sound of their call as you internally or audibly state your intention. This coupling of visualization and intention-setting can act as a potent primer for the meditation, creating a vibrational match between you and the energy of the corvid realm.

Reinforcing Intentions Post-Meditation

Setting an intention is not just a pre-meditation practice. It's important to also revisit your intention after the meditation is complete. Take a few moments to reflect on your experiences and insights during the meditation and how they relate to your initial intention. You might even consider jotting down your thoughts in a journal for further reflection and to track your progress over time.

In summary, setting an intention is an invaluable step in your meditative practice, more so when you aim to connect with the mystical and fascinating realm of corvids. Your intention serves as a guiding light, illuminating the path of your inner journey. By aligning your mind, heart, and spirit towards a focused inquiry, you create a conduit for the wisdom and messages that the corvid realm has to share. This practice of setting an intention thus enriches not only your meditation but also your broader understanding and relationship with these extraordinary beings.

CHAPTER 6: BASIC MEDITATION TECHNIQUES

6.1 MINDFULNESS MEDITATION

In this chapter, we explore the cornerstone of many meditation practices—mindfulness meditation—and how it can be specifically applied to deepen your connection with the fascinating world of corvids. Mindfulness, a concept rooted in Buddhist teachings, has been embraced worldwide for its power to cultivate self-awareness, reduce stress, and enrich our experience of life. As we guide you through this mindfulness journey, we invite you to channel this focused awareness toward your interaction with crows and other corvids, whether they are part of your immediate environment or creatures you engage with spiritually.

The Essence of Mindfulness

The practice of mindfulness meditation requires centering one's attention on the here-and-now without attaching one's self to any particular interpretation of what one sees. Typically, one begins by focusing on their breath, bodily sensations, or an external object. The key is to allow the experience to unfold naturally, simply observing thoughts and sensations without getting tangled in them. As for its applicability to our subject, observing crows can serve as an effective external point of focus in mindfulness practice.

Many find that crows, with their perceptive eyes and inquisitive behavior, offer an engaging focus for observation. Their actions in the present moment—whether they are foraging, communicating with each other, or simply perched in quietude—can draw you into a mindful state. As you do so, you'll notice that the chatter of the mind begins to subside, allowing you to delve deeper into the understanding of these complex beings.

Setting Up Your Practice

When you're planning to practice mindfulness meditation with crows, it's helpful to find a peaceful environment where you can observe these birds without too much distraction. Choose a comfortable seat, either indoors near a window overlooking an area frequented by crows, or outdoors where you can sit quietly without disturbing their natural behavior. Once you've settled in, start by taking a few deep breaths, grounding yourself in the present moment.

From here, let your gaze naturally settle on a crow or a group of crows. You don't have to strain to keep your eyes open; rather, adopt a soft gaze, as if you are absorbing the entire scene before you. Begin by simply observing them—the way they move, the colors in their feathers, the way they interact with their surroundings and each other.

Mindfulness in Action: Observing Corvid Behavior

As you watch, maintain an open awareness. Allow your thoughts to come and go freely, but don't latch on to them. When your mind does wander, gently bring your attention back to the birds before you. You may start to notice small details that you would typically overlook, like the meticulous way a crow uses its beak to forage or the nuanced calls exchanged between two individuals. This form of observation is not passive; it's an active, enriching experience that enhances your intuitive understanding of corvid behavior.

Over time, you may also find that this practice cultivates a deeper emotional or spiritual connection with crows. They are, after all, beings with complex social structures and problem-solving abilities, and a consistent mindfulness practice can pave the way for more profound interactions, both observed and felt.

Bridging Mindfulness and Spirituality

One of the beautiful aspects of mindfulness is its versatility. For those who are more spiritually inclined, mindfulness can serve as an entry point into deeper spiritual experiences with crows. The acute awareness cultivated through mindfulness can prepare your mind to receive intuitive insights or messages, often thought to be gifts from the corvid realm. While the scientific rigor may not wholly support these experiences, they are nonetheless meaningful to many individuals who find spiritual companionship and guidance from their engagements with these remarkable birds.

To summarize, mindfulness meditation offers a gateway to a deeper understanding and connection with the world of crows. By grounding ourselves in the present moment and focusing our awareness, we not only enrich our observational skills but also open ourselves up to the possibility of more profound, even spiritual, interactions with these fascinating creatures. Whether you are watching a crow soar through the sky, listening to their unique calls, or simply feeling their presence in your immediate environment, mindfulness invites you to experience these moments fully, enriching your ongoing journey through the mystical and captivating realm of corvids.

6.2 GUIDED MEDITATION

Guided meditation is a form of mental exercise that involves following a set narrative or script, often led by a trained guide or teacher, to achieve specific goals such as relaxation, clarity, or connection with a particular subject. In the context of this book, guided meditation serves as a powerful conduit for linking your consciousness with the corvid realm. This chapter will elucidate the nuances of guided meditation, particularly focusing on its effectiveness in helping you establish a deeper connection with the fascinating world of corvids.

The Mechanics of Guided Meditation

Unlike mindfulness meditation, where the focus is primarily on your breath or on being present, guided meditation takes you on a structured journey through your imagination. Typically, the meditation starts with relaxation techniques to calm the mind and body. You are then led through a series of visualizations or prompts that facilitate your connection with the intended focus —in our case, the corvid realm. This could involve imagining yourself in a serene forest where you encounter a crow, which then leads you to an insightful conversation or a mutual energetic exchange. The guide's words serve as a roadmap, helping you navigate your mental and emotional landscape while also providing a storyline that brings the subject of your meditation to life.

Scientific Validation

The effectiveness of guided meditation is not just anecdotal; it has been studied in various scientific settings. Research suggests that guided meditation can improve mental well-being, reduce stress, and enhance cognitive functions. Although these studies often do not directly investigate the connection with corvids, the generalized findings support the notion that guided meditation can be a powerful tool for establishing a conscious link with specific subjects.

Specific Techniques for Connecting with Corvids

When it comes to guided meditation that focuses on connecting with corvids, the imagination becomes your primary instrument. Begin by centering yourself through deep breathing exercises and let the guide's words draw you into a detailed imaginary landscape where you may encounter crows or other corvids. Use your senses—sight, sound, touch, even taste and smell—to enrich your imagined experience. Here are some techniques to help you in this journey:

Visualize a Gathering: Imagine a peaceful assembly of crows and other corvids in a serene location like a forest clearing or a lakeside. Visualize yourself approaching them and being warmly welcomed.

Engage in Telepathic Conversations: Once you feel comfortable and welcomed in your imagined setting, try to engage the corvids in a mental dialogue. Ask them questions or wait for messages they might have for you.

Mutual Energy Exchange: In your meditation, you might envision a luminescent thread of energy connecting you with the crow. Imagine that this energy exchange is symbiotic, offering clarity, wisdom, or simply a sense of deep connection.

Safeguarding Your Experience

Just as with any meditative practice, it's crucial to ensure you're in a safe and comfortable space where you won't be disturbed. Guided meditation often takes you into a deeply relaxed state; hence, it's advisable to sit or lie down in a position that supports this level of relaxation. Make sure to come out of the meditation gently, taking time to ground yourself back in your physical surroundings.

Final Thoughts

Guided meditation is a versatile and effective method for not only enhancing your mental and emotional well-being but also for forming a meaningful connection with the corvid realm. Through structured narrative and imagination, it allows you to explore and deepen your relationship with these incredible beings. Whether you seek wisdom, companionship, or a greater understanding of the world around you, guided meditation offers a structured pathway for those aims. So the next time you feel the call of a crow or spot one perched mysteriously on a tree, consider embarking on a guided meditation to explore the deeper message that these captivating creatures may hold for you.

6.3 MANTRAS AND AFFIRMATIONS

The value of mantras and affirmations in meditation is often underappreciated. Yet, these simple yet profound utterances can have a tremendous impact on one's meditative journey. In the context of connecting with the corvid realm, mantras and affirmations offer a tool for deepening the relationship between human consciousness and the intelligence of these fascinating birds.

The Power of Mantras

Mantras are essentially words or phrases that are repeated either aloud or internally during meditation. They come from ancient traditions—most notably Hinduism and Buddhism—but have found a home in various spiritual and religious practices globally. Mantras can be in Sanskrit, the ancient language often used in spiritual texts, or they can be in any language that the practitioner feels comfortable with. The purpose of a mantra is to assist in focusing the mind and facilitating a deeper state of awareness.

Mantras related to corvids could draw from their various attributes such as intelligence, adaptability, or symbolic meanings. For instance, one might choose a mantra like "Wisdom of the Crow, guide me," repeated either internally or externally. The effect is a reinforcement of the intent to connect with the insight that crows can offer, thereby deepening your meditation experience.

Understanding Affirmations

Affirmations are slightly different from mantras but serve a similar purpose. They are positive statements intended to challenge and control self-sabotaging thoughts or behaviors. Unlike mantras, affirmations are usually complete sentences aimed at creating a specific outcome, and they are almost always articulated in the practitioner's native language. When applied to meditations aimed at connecting with the corvid realm, affirmations can help establish a mindset conducive to open, meaningful interactions with these remarkable birds.

Affirmations might sound like, "I am open to the messages that crows bring," or "I am part of the intricate web of life that includes all beings, including crows." These affirmations set the stage for a meditative experience that invites not just focus but also transformative thinking.

Combining Mantras and Affirmations in Meditation

A balanced approach might be to integrate both mantras and affirmations into your meditative practice. Starting your meditation with an affirmation can set your intention clearly and prepare your mind for the experience. Following this, the use of a mantra throughout your meditation can help maintain focus and deepen your awareness.

To merge this with the previous techniques discussed in this book, such as mindfulness and guided meditations, you might start with a few deep breaths and an affirmation. As you proceed into mindfulness or guided meditation, the mantra can serve as a grounding element, helping to keep the mind from wandering and reinforcing your connection with the corvid realm.

Cultural and Personal Sensitivity

It is crucial to approach the use of mantras and affirmations with a sense of cultural and personal sensitivity. If you choose to use mantras from specific cultural or religious backgrounds, be respectful of their origins and meanings. Make sure that your adoption of such phrases does not amount to cultural appropriation, and if possible, understand the deeper meanings and contexts behind them.

The same applies to affirmations. Make them personal and meaningful to you. When connecting with the corvid realm, the aim is to facilitate a two-way interaction based on mutual respect and understanding. Therefore, the mantras and affirmations you choose should reflect that intent, aligning you with the energy and intelligence of crows.

In summary, mantras and affirmations can add a valuable dimension to your meditative practices aimed at connecting with the corvid realm. Whether you are whispering ancient Sanskrit phrases or mentally repeating affirmations that resonate with you, these techniques can serve as potent tools for focus and transformation. Their incorporation into your practice can deepen not only your state of mind but also your relational understanding of these intelligent birds, opening new doors for interaction and wisdom-sharing.

CHAPTER 7: ADVANCED MEDITATIVE PRACTICES

7.1 SHAMANIC JOURNEYING

Shamanic journeying represents a pathway that merges ancient spiritual traditions with the mystical allure of the corvid realm. This advanced meditative technique enables a deeply personal and transformative connection with corvids, drawing upon practices that transcend time and geographical boundaries. Rooted in ancient shamanic traditions, this method allows us to explore the various dimensions of our existence, including our relationship with nature and the animal kingdom. For those intrigued by the profound wisdom and symbolic messages of corvids, shamanic journeying offers an experiential landscape that is deeply enriching.

What is Shamanic Journeying?

Shamanic journeying is a form of meditation that stems from practices associated with indigenous and ancestral spiritual traditions. Typically guided by rhythmic drumming or other repetitive sounds, practitioners enter altered states of consciousness that facilitate communication with spirit guides, ancestors, and other realms of existence. In this specific context, the goal is to engage meaningfully with the spiritual essence or energy of corvids, unveiling messages or insights that are personally or universally significant.

The Role of the Shamanic Drum

One of the critical elements of shamanic journeying is the use of the drum. The drum's rhythmic beat serves as a sonic vehicle, transporting the journeyer into non-ordinary states of reality. These are realms where spirit animals, guides, and transformative experiences are encountered. The drum's beat is considered the "heartbeat" of the Earth, aligning us with the natural world and making the connection with corvids more intimate and potent.

Preparation for the Journey

Before embarking on a shamanic journey to connect with the corvid realm, it's essential to prepare adequately. Clear intentions must be set, focusing on the questions you'd like answered or the wisdom you seek to gain from the experience. Creating a sacred space, as discussed in previous chapters, helps facilitate a deeper connection. Many practitioners also choose to incorporate elements that relate to crows or other corvids—be it feathers, images, or other symbolic items—to strengthen the focus and clarity of the journey.

Steps in Shamanic Journeying

Setting the Space: This involves creating an environment conducive to deep meditation. It may include lighting a candle, setting up an altar, or smudging the area with sage.

The Call: Once comfortable, the practitioner uses a drum or recorded drumming audio to initiate the journey. The journey typically begins with a call to the spirit of the crow or other corvid entities, inviting them into the sacred space.

Entering the Realm: As the rhythm of the drum continues, the journeyer allows themselves to enter an altered state where they may encounter various forms of symbolism, messages, or experiences.

Communication: Once in the corvid realm, direct or symbolic communication can occur. Some people report seeing vivid landscapes, others converse with the corvid spirits, while some experience sensations or emotions.

Returning: After a set period, the drumming changes its rhythm, signaling it's time to return from the journey. The practitioner should gradually bring their awareness back to their physical surroundings and take some time to integrate the experience.

Ethical Considerations

Though this practice is deeply personal, it's important to approach it with sensitivity and respect for the cultures from which shamanic journeying originates. As a form of spiritual exploration, it necessitates responsible conduct, both ethically and culturally. Avoid appropriating practices from cultures to which you do not belong, and always maintain a reverential attitude toward the entities and energies you encounter.

Shamanic journeying offers an intricate, nuanced way to connect with the corvid realm. It provides a channel to explore the wisdom, messages, and symbology that these enigmatic birds have to offer. However, as with any deep spiritual practice, it requires preparation, intention, and, above all, respect. This method allows us not just to understand corvids better but also to foster a stronger connection with the natural world, inviting us to delve into the intricate web of relationships that define our existence.

7.2 ASTRAL PROJECTION

Astral projection is a term that has intrigued, confounded, and fascinated spiritual seekers and researchers for centuries. Although it might seem quite esoteric, it's a practice that many claim to have experienced, describing it as an out-of-body experience where one's consciousness or "astral body" travels outside the physical body. It's a concept that has been explored in various religious and philosophical traditions, and there are differing perspectives on what exactly happens during the experience. The astral plane is often viewed as a different dimension, an extension of the physical world but less limited by the laws of time and space.

The Connection to Corvids

While astral projection is not inherently linked to corvids, it offers a unique platform for possible interaction and communication with these intriguing birds. The elusive and mystical nature of corvids, combined with their documented intelligence and ability to recognize and remember humans, opens the door to intriguing possibilities. During an astral journey, you could visualize meeting a crow or raven as your guide, leading you through various landscapes, teaching you new perspectives, or sharing wisdom.

Astral Projection Techniques

It's important to approach astral projection with respect, intent, and a good understanding of the process. There are several methods to achieve astral projection, but most include variations of relaxation, focus, and visualization.

Relaxation: Lie down in a comfortable position in a space where you will not be disturbed. Close your eyes and focus on your breath. Gradually, attempt to enter a state of deep relaxation, allowing all your muscles to release tension.

Focus: Once relaxed, shift your focus inward. Some practitioners use techniques like imagining a rope that they climb, or a door they walk through. This aids in transitioning from a state of physical awareness to astral readiness.

Visualization: As you sense your consciousness loosening from your physical body, you can start to visualize the environment or experience you want to have. This is where you might integrate your intent to meet a crow or another corvid as your guide.

The Journey: If successful, you will feel as though you have entered a different state or plane. Here, you can interact with your crow guide, seeking wisdom or insights, or merely observing the surroundings.

Return: At the end of your astral journey, gently bring your focus back to your physical body. This often happens naturally, but visualizing a return path or simply willing it can be helpful. Take some moments to ground yourself before moving.

Safety and Precautions

Given that astral projection often involves deep states of relaxation and focus, it's crucial to be aware of a few safety guidelines:

Be in a secure, quiet environment where you won't be disturbed.

If you have any medical conditions, particularly those affecting your heart or breathing, consult a healthcare professional before attempting astral projection.

Maintain a neutral or positive emotional state. Negative emotions can create an unsettling experience.

Combining Astral Projection with Previous Techniques

If you've been following along with the other chapters in this book, you might wonder how astral projection fits into the overall practice of meditating with crows. Essentially, it serves as an advanced technique, adding another layer of depth to your encounters with the corvid realm. You can combine astral projection with mindfulness meditation or even shamanic journeying to create a multifaceted experience.

In summary, astral projection offers a fascinating and profound method for potentially connecting with the enigmatic world of corvids. Whether seeking wisdom or simply curious about this spiritual practice, astral projection can become a valuable addition to your spiritual toolkit. Like any other form of meditation or spiritual exploration, it demands respect, intent, and an open mind. And who knows, your astral journeys may provide yet another way for you to unlock the complex layers of understanding and respect between humans and corvids.

7.3 LUCID DREAMING

Lucid dreaming, a state in which dreamers become aware that they are dreaming, offers a unique platform for interaction with the corvid realm. While in a lucid dream, you can consciously decide to seek out crows or other corvids and engage with them in ways that may not be possible in waking reality. The dream state can serve as an alternate dimension where the barriers between the human and corvid realms are more porous, allowing for richer, more meaningful interactions.

What is Lucid Dreaming?

Lucid dreaming is a term coined by Dutch psychiatrist Frederik van Eeden in 1913, although the concept itself has been around for much longer, dating back to ancient Tibetan practices. In a lucid dream, you are aware that you are dreaming and can exert some level of control over the dream environment, characters, and narrative. Researchers like Stephen LaBerge have conducted various studies to explore the mechanisms and potential applications of lucid dreaming. LaBerge, in particular, used techniques like "reality testing" to help individuals become aware within their dreams.

The Connection Between Lucid Dreaming and the Corvid Realm

Dreams are seen as one of the most direct routes to the subconscious mind, an arena filled with symbols, archetypes, and often, animal totems. Crows and other corvids often appear in dreams as messengers or guides, reflecting either external truths or internal wisdom that may be elusive in waking life. When you become lucid in a dream featuring a crow, you have the opportunity to engage directly with this powerful symbol, asking questions or seeking guidance. Many practitioners report experiencing profound insights during such encounters.

Techniques for Lucid Dreaming

While there are numerous techniques for inducing lucidity, some are particularly conducive to connecting with the corvid realm.

Dream Journaling: Keeping a dream journal helps you recognize recurring themes and symbols, making it easier to become aware in future dreams. Noting instances where crows appear can be especially beneficial.

Reality Testing: Throughout the day, ask yourself, "Am I dreaming?" and perform a simple test like trying to push your finger through your palm. The habit will carry over into your dreams, increasing the likelihood of becoming lucid.

Mnemonic Induction of Lucid Dreams (MILD): Before falling asleep, repeat a phrase like "The next time I dream, I will realize I am dreaming." This can prime your mind to become aware in the dream state.

Wake Back to Bed (WBTB): This involves waking up about five hours after falling asleep, staying awake for a short period, and then going back to sleep. This technique heightens your awareness and increases the chances of lucidity.

Interacting with Corvids in Lucid Dreams

Once you become lucid, you can actively seek out interactions with crows or other corvids. You may find them perched in dream landscapes or flying overhead. Approach them respectfully, as you would in waking life. You can ask questions or simply observe their behavior. Remember to maintain a posture of openness and receptivity. You can even try mimicking their calls or extending a "gift" as a sign of goodwill. The experiences can range from whimsical and uplifting to deeply spiritual, often depending on your initial intention.

Scientific and Spiritual Implications

Though still a budding field, research on lucid dreaming suggests that the practice can have therapeutic applications, ranging from treating nightmares to enhancing creativity. When it comes to connecting with the corvid realm, lucid dreaming can serve both as a spiritual exercise and a form of experiential learning. The symbolic nature of crows, deeply entrenched in various cultural and spiritual contexts, can add a layer of significance to these dream interactions.

In summary, lucid dreaming opens up a fascinating avenue for connecting with the corvid realm. While the scientific community continues to investigate the possibilities and mechanics of lucid dreaming, spiritual practitioners see in it a path to a more profound understanding of these mysterious birds as well as a meaningful method to communicate with them. Techniques like dream journaling and reality testing can facilitate lucidity, providing you with a conscious platform to seek out and engage with crows in a dream landscape. These experiences, rich in symbolism and personal significance, can offer insights that are both profoundly spiritual and practically applicable.

CHAPTER 8: PRACTICAL APPLICATIONS

8.1 DAILY LIFE

Meditations and messages from the corvid realm can be remarkably transformative, not just in spiritual endeavors but also in day-to-day life. While it might be easy to compartmentalize the mystical and practical aspects of our existence, the wisdom gleaned from our feathery friends encourages us to blur those lines. In this chapter, we delve into how the spiritual practices and insights discussed so far can significantly influence and enhance various aspects of daily life, from personal well-being to interpersonal relationships and decision-making.

Mindfulness and Presence

One of the first impacts you might notice when integrating corvid-inspired meditations into your life is a heightened sense of mindfulness. The simple act of observing crows in nature can be an exercise in grounding oneself in the present moment. This presence often translates into other aspects of life, making you more attuned to your immediate environment, whether it's appreciating the nuances in a conversation or noticing the details in a piece of art. This heightened awareness can make daily activities more enjoyable and fulfilling.

Stress Management

Crows are often observed as resilient and adaptable creatures. They are rarely seen panicking, even when faced with potential threats or challenges. Emulating this quality can offer a powerful form of stress management. When incorporated into regular meditation practices, the symbolic representation of a crow can serve as a reminder to approach difficulties with calm and calculated focus rather than stress or anxiety. Visualizing a crow during challenging times can be an effective way to center oneself and find clarity, making the situation more manageable.

Decision-Making

Crows are famous for their problem-solving abilities. In scientific studies, they have been observed using tools, recognizing human faces, and even understanding the concept of water displacement. The ingenuity of crows can serve as a model for human decision-making. While it might seem far-fetched, taking a moment to ponder "what would a crow do?" can offer a fresh perspective when faced with complex decisions. This approach encourages creative problem-solving, a skill that can be invaluable in daily life, whether you're deciding on a career move or finding a solution to a personal dilemma.

Interpersonal Relationships

The social structures of corvid communities are intricate and collaborative. Their ability to cooperate in tasks like foraging and defense can offer insights into improving our human relationships. Being mindful of the needs and emotional states of those around you, much like crows do within their communities, fosters more meaningful and enriching relationships. Also, crows maintain long-term bonds and display emotions akin to empathy, qualities that can guide us in nurturing long-lasting, supportive relationships in our lives.

Environmental Awareness

Engaging with the corvid realm through meditation and observation also makes one more sensitive to the environment. This awareness goes beyond merely appreciating nature—it encourages a more conscious lifestyle. The tenacity of crows in adapting to various environments can inspire individuals to adopt more sustainable practices in daily life. Whether it's being more mindful of waste or opting for eco-friendly products, these small changes make a substantial collective impact.

In summary, the teachings from the corvid realm are not confined to moments of spiritual practice but are interwoven into the fabric of daily life. They offer a toolkit for enhanced mindfulness, stress management, decision-making, interpersonal relationships, and environmental awareness. So the next time you spot a crow on your morning walk or during a quiet afternoon, remember that its presence is not just a fleeting encounter but a subtle reminder of the enriched life that awaits you when you bring its wisdom into your everyday experience.

8.2 RELATIONSHIPS

The mystical teachings of the crow realm may initially seem far removed from the everyday challenges of human relationships. Yet, it's astonishing how corvid wisdom can provide valuable insights into our interactions with others. Much like crows, humans thrive on social connections, community, and communication. Here, we explore how the practices and principles that stem from your meditations with crows can guide you in navigating the complexities of relationships, whether with family, friends, or romantic partners.

Emotional Intelligence and Awareness

One of the first things we can learn from crows is the value of emotional intelligence. These birds have been observed displaying empathy and cooperation in their social interactions. As you dive deeper into your meditative practice, you may find yourself becoming more attuned to the emotional currents that flow through your relationships. Just as crows pick up on subtle cues from their community, you'll begin to notice subtle non-verbal signals from the people around you. Understanding these emotional nuances can help in maintaining a balanced relationship, and can be particularly beneficial during conflict resolution.

Communication: Listening and Speaking

Crows are highly skilled communicators, employing a wide array of calls for different situations. In human terms, this translates into the ability to express oneself clearly and listen attentively. Through your meditations, you may come to recognize the importance of not just speaking your truth, but also truly hearing what the other person is saying. The talent of active listening is one that must be honed over time but can be life-changing when it comes to better comprehending interpersonal conflicts and finding solutions to those conflicts. Just as crows adapt their communication techniques according to their needs, mastering the art of verbal and non-verbal communication in relationships can go a long way in building meaningful connections.

Setting Boundaries

Observing crows, one quickly realizes that they are territorial birds who are clear about their boundaries. Humans can learn much from this. It's crucial in any relationship to establish and respect boundaries, ensuring that the interactions are built on mutual respect and understanding. Your meditative practices may assist you in becoming more aware of what your boundaries are and how to communicate them effectively to your partner, family, or friends. Knowing one's boundaries and respecting those of others creates a healthy space where a relationship can flourish.

Problem-Solving and Adaptability

Crows are incredibly resourceful birds that are often seen

using tools or coming up with creative solutions to challenges. In relationships, challenges are inevitable. What makes a relationship resilient is the ability to adapt and find solutions to problems as they arise. Your spiritual practice and connection with the corvid realm could grant you a unique perspective for resolving issues. By applying the same level of creativity and resourcefulness observed in crows, you can breathe new life into how you handle relationship challenges, turning obstacles into opportunities for growth and deeper understanding.

The Alchemy of Relationships

The symbolism of crows often alludes to transformation and alchemy. Similarly, relationships can be a transformative experience that allows us to grow, change, and become better versions of ourselves. If you imbue your relationships with the wisdom gathered from your corvid meditations, you set the stage for a mutually enriching experience. Just as crows collectively solve problems and share resources, a relationship built on open communication, emotional intelligence, clear boundaries, and mutual growth can only be described as alchemical in its ability to transform both individuals involved.

In summary, the mystical insights gained from your connection with the corvid realm are not just isolated spiritual experiences. They can be deeply ingrained into the fabric of your human relationships, providing a well-rounded approach to emotional intelligence, communication, boundary-setting, problem-solving, and transformation. As you continue on your spiritual journey with crows, these lessons can serve as guiding principles, enriching not only your own life but also the lives of those you hold dear.

8.3 CAREER AND CREATIVITY

The whispers of wisdom from the corvid realm are not confined to spiritual enlightenment or personal relationships alone; they reverberate through the corridors of our professional lives and creative endeavors as well. As curious as it may sound, paying attention to the messages and inspirations derived from these intelligent beings can offer unique insights into your career path, enhance your creativity, and bring a fresh perspective to problem-solving.

Corvid-Inspired Problem-Solving

We already know from previous chapters that corvids are expert problem solvers, capable of creating tools and solving complex puzzles to access food. This can serve as a metaphor in our professional lives. When faced with complex tasks or challenges, one might take inspiration from a crow's approach: observing the situation quietly from various angles before taking decisive, and often innovative, action. The crow doesn't allow barriers to become blockades; it finds a way to work around them. Similarly, we can incorporate this adaptability into our decision-making processes. Whether you're a manager trying to navigate team dynamics or an artist struggling with a creative block, this "corvid approach" can help you perceive problems as puzzles to be solved rather than obstacles to be avoided.

Intuition and Decision-Making

Corvids also rely on a certain level of intuition to survive. This intuitive approach is something we can incorporate into our career decisions. Often, the best decisions come from a balance of logical reasoning and gut feeling, a blend of the mind's analytics and the heart's intuition. Meditation practices focused on corvids can help one tap into this intuition, offering a form of guidance that may be beneficial when making critical choices in your professional life.

Creative Catalyst

Creativity isn't just about producing art; it's an integral part of innovation in any field. One of the unique qualities of corvids is their natural curiosity and playfulness. They can be seen sliding down snowy roofs for fun or playing catch-me-if-you-can in the air. This playful approach to life can be an immense catalyst for creativity. In moments where you feel stuck or uninspired, stepping back and embracing a playful attitude can provide a fresh perspective and potentially lead to breakthroughs. Meditation practices that involve envisioning yourself as a crow, soaring freely through the skies, can help unlock this playful creativity within you.

Embracing Failure as Learning

Crows and ravens are not always successful in their endeavors, but they learn from their failures. Whether it's an unsuccessful attempt to crack open a nut or navigate social interactions within their community, corvids take these experiences as learning opportunities. This approach can be incredibly beneficial in our careers, where fear of failure often holds us back. Rather than viewing setbacks as indicators of your limitations, seeing them as stepping stones toward mastery can be empowering. This mind-shift, inspired by our feathered friends, can be nurtured through mindfulness practices and reflections on the corvid realm.

Harmonizing Work-Life Balance

Finally, corvids lead a balanced life that involves not just work in the form of foraging and nest-building, but also social interactions and play. This is a valuable lesson for modern humans, who often find it challenging to maintain a healthy work-life balance. Messages from the corvid realm can serve as a reminder to infuse elements of play and social connection into our busy schedules, thereby contributing to a more balanced and fulfilling life.

In summary, the wisdom imparted by the corvid realm has the potential to enrich not just our personal lives but our professional and creative pursuits as well. Through adopting a corvid-inspired approach to problem-solving, honing our intuition, catalyzing creativity, learning from failures, and maintaining a balanced life, we can navigate the complexities of our careers with greater ease and fulfillment. Just as the crow finds its way through a myriad of challenges, so too can we find our own unique paths in the professional and creative landscapes.

CHAPTER 9: CASE STUDIES

9.1 Personal Narratives

In our exploration of the mystical and intellectual realms of corvids, it can be profoundly enriching to hear firsthand accounts of those who have ventured into this captivating world. The beauty of personal narratives lies in their ability to give us a human touch, allowing us to experience the phenomena we've discussed through someone else's eyes. The stories shared here demonstrate how various meditation techniques, symbolic interpretations, and spiritual practices involving corvids have led to personal transformation.

The Artist and the Crow's Feather

Clara, a visual artist in her late thirties, was initially drawn to the aesthetic elegance of crows. She decided to practice mindfulness meditation with the aim of focusing on the details of crows—be it their feathers, their eyes, or their movements. Clara soon noticed a peculiar event; she found a crow feather in her art studio, a place she believed to be free from any intrusion by birds. Interpreting this as a sign, Clara began incorporating crow imagery and feathers into her artwork. Within months, she discovered a fresh sense of creativity and began a series of art installations inspired by corvids, which eventually earned her recognition in her local art community.

The Engineer and the Crow Calls

Jacob, a civil engineer, had a different yet equally compelling story. While he was always appreciative of nature, he never had a specific inclination toward crows. Jacob began practicing guided meditation focused on listening to the calls of crows after reading about their complex communication systems. At a pivotal moment in his career, he found himself waking up to the sound of crow calls that led him to a moment of reflection and ultimately a significant career decision. Taking it as a meaningful synchronicity, he switched career paths and reported feeling more fulfilled than ever before.

The Mystic and Crow Synchronicities

Sophia, who identifies as a mystic, took her interaction with crows to an advanced spiritual level. She practiced shamanic journeying to connect deeply with the corvid realm. Sophia claimed that during these journeys, she received visions that offered her deep personal insights and transformative wisdom. She mentioned experiencing an increasing number of synchronicities involving crows after each journey. These events served as affirmations for her to continue her spiritual practices. Sophia now conducts workshops, combining her wisdom and techniques to help others explore their own spiritual dimensions through interactions with corvids.

The Biologist and Problem-Solving Crows

Lastly, let's consider Daniel, a biologist, who turned his scientific curiosity into a form of meditation. Focused on observing the problem-solving skills of crows, Daniel spent time watching these birds in their natural habitat. He translated his observations into a mindful practice, where he would meditate upon the complexities of corvid behavior. This not only enriched his academic research but also brought him a newfound respect and a deeper emotional connection with these intelligent creatures.

Summary

Each of these narratives is a testament to the multifaceted interactions humans can have with the corvid realm. These stories, divergent in their origins and motivations, converge on similar outcomes: personal transformation and a deepened connection with the natural world. Whether you find yourself aligned more with Clara, Jacob, Sophia, or Daniel, the possibilities for meaningful engagement with corvids are varied and endlessly enriching. While these personal narratives can't be generalized as universal truths, they offer precious glimpses into the individual journeys that collectively enrich our understanding of what it means to connect spiritually, intellectually, and emotionally with the remarkable world of corvids.

9.2 SCIENTIFIC STUDIES

The idea that crows and other corvids are more than just random birds soaring across the sky has long been a subject of fascination. While earlier chapters delved into personal narratives and mythological aspects of these remarkable birds, this chapter takes a scholarly turn. We will review scientific studies that add an evidence-based dimension to the awe and wonder inspired by crows. These studies not only affirm the folklore and individual experiences discussed in previous chapters but also reveal unique insights into corvid intelligence, behavior, and interaction with humans.

Cognitive Abilities and Problem-Solving

One of the most compelling areas of research concerning corvids is their cognitive ability. Studies carried out by academics like Dr. Alex Taylor at the University of Cambridge reveal that New Caledonian crows are capable of carrying out activities that were hitherto thought to be solely the purview of humans and higher primates. For example, these crows have been observed using sticks to extract insects from tree barks, demonstrating not just tool use, but also tool creation—a skill indicative of advanced cognitive functions.

This scientific observation correlates with the personal

experiences of many who find crows to be extraordinarily intelligent and adaptable. Tool use is not just a random act but a calculated one, requiring an understanding of cause and effect, planning, and even the ability to foresee a problem before it arises. Such findings lend scientific credence to the idea that crows could indeed be potential messengers or guides, capable of complex thought processes.

Social Dynamics and Communication

In the realm of social interaction, corvids also demonstrate complex behaviors that are subjects of extensive research. Dr. John Marzluff, a professor of wildlife science at the University of Washington, conducted studies indicating that crows have the ability to recognize individual human faces and communicate this information among their flock. This facial recognition ability, also evidenced through controlled experiments, suggests a level of social cognition that adds a new layer to our understanding of these birds.

The advanced communication skills among corvids provide a scientific backdrop to their intricate social structures, discussed in personal narratives and mythologies. These findings suggest that the 'messages' from crows could be part of a more intricate system of communication, making the concept of meditating with these birds a more plausible practice than skeptics might assume.

Interactions with Humans

Beyond their cognitive and social skills, corvids have been observed to interact with humans in ways that defy simple explanations. Studies have shown that crows can form bonds with people who feed them regularly, going so far as to bring back 'gifts' like shiny objects as tokens of appreciation. Such behaviors lend weight to the concept of a deeper, perhaps even spiritual, connection between humans and crows, a notion supported by the many personal experiences recounted in earlier chapters.

Environmental Adaptability

Corvids are not only intelligent but also extraordinarily adaptable, as evidenced by their ability to thrive in various environments —from forests to urban settings. Researchers have studied how corvids adjust their diets and social behaviors depending on their habitats, further highlighting their intelligence and adaptability. These traits make them ideal subjects for meditation and spiritual practices that involve connecting with the natural world, as their adaptability could symbolize resilience and flexibility—qualities that are beneficial in human life.

Synthesizing Scientific and Personal Perspectives

The scientific studies on corvids confirm and expand upon the themes explored through personal narratives and symbolic interpretations. Their advanced cognitive skills, complex social dynamics, peculiar interactions with humans, and adaptability to various environments validate the mystique and reverence surrounding these birds. While the scientific approach may initially seem at odds with the more spiritual or mystical views, they actually complement each other, offering a multifaceted understanding of crows that enriches our interactions with them.

In summary, the world of corvid research offers an array of findings that support and deepen the spiritual and symbolic perspectives discussed in previous chapters. Whether you're a skeptic seeking empirical proof or a believer in the mystical attributes of these birds, the body of scientific work on corvids provides compelling evidence that these are not just ordinary birds, but creatures of significant intelligence and complexity, worthy of our attention and respect.

9.3 EXPERT OPINIONS

This chapter delves into the viewpoints of experts in various fields —spiritual leaders, shamans, and scientists—providing a well-rounded understanding of the mystical and intellectual realm of corvids. Each of these perspectives not only complements but enriches the previous discussions on meditating with crows and understanding their significance in our lives.

Spiritual Leaders on Corvid Wisdom

Spiritual leaders often regard corvids as sentient beings with wisdom that transcends the barriers of language and species. They talk about the crow's role in ancient scriptures and spiritual teachings, signifying transformation, magic, and the dichotomy of life and death. Several Eastern and Western spiritual traditions incorporate the crow as a messenger between the divine and the human world.

In Tibetan Buddhism, for instance, the crow is seen as a protector and messenger for the deities. In Native American spirituality, the crow is often a symbol of creation and transformation. These interpretations align closely with the teachings on mindfulness and spiritual presence that many of these spiritual leaders advocate, suggesting that the wisdom of corvids can be accessible to us when we enter a state of meditative awareness.

Shamans and the Corvid Realm

Shamans, who engage in practices to interact with the spirit world, also acknowledge the corvid realm's unique mystical aspects. According to shamanic traditions, corvids, particularly crows and ravens, are "spirit animals" that can guide individuals in their spiritual journeys. These experts often use drumming, ritualistic dances, and other forms of active meditation to connect with the corvid realm. They interpret the cawing of crows, their flight patterns, and even their interactions with other animals as spiritual messages. Some shamans regard crows as keepers of sacred law, beings who know the cosmic order's intricacies and can offer guidance in understanding the world's spiritual architecture.

Scientific Perspective on Corvid Intelligence

Science adds another layer to our understanding of crows and their capabilities. Researchers specializing in animal behavior and cognition have conducted numerous studies confirming the advanced problem-solving abilities of corvids. Experiments reveal that crows can recognize human faces, understand the concept of water displacement, and even use tools—skills previously believed to be unique to humans and certain primates.

Cognitive scientists and ornithologists often use the term "corvid cognition" to describe these capabilities, drawing parallels between human intelligence and corvid intelligence. The data from these studies suggest that crows possess a form of consciousness, raising compelling ethical considerations about their treatment and the protection of their habitats.

Bridging the Gap

Interestingly, there is an emerging field of scholars and practitioners who aim to bridge the gap between the spiritual and scientific perspectives on corvids. They argue for an integrative approach that considers both the mystical wisdom and empirical evidence surrounding these fascinating birds. By understanding the corvid realm through multiple lenses, one can form a richer, more nuanced relationship with these creatures, tapping into their wisdom for personal growth and transformation.

Summary

Expert opinions on the mystical and intellectual aspects of corvids are as diverse as they are enriching. Whether you lean towards the spiritual insights offered by spiritual leaders and shamans or prefer the empirically grounded findings from scientific studies, the different viewpoints provide a well-rounded framework for understanding these intriguing birds. As you venture further into your journey with the corvid realm, these expert opinions can serve as guideposts, illuminating your path with multifaceted wisdom.

CHAPTER 10: COMMON CHALLENGES AND SOLUTIONS

10.1 SKEPTICISM AND DOUBT

The road to the mystical realm of corvids, as this book details, can be thrilling yet challenging. One of the foremost challenges that aspiring spiritual seekers and corvid enthusiasts may face is skepticism and doubt. In this chapter, we'll delve into the possible origins of these doubts, how they manifest, and practical ways to address them.

Cognitive Dissonance and Belief Systems

One of the significant reasons behind skepticism is cognitive dissonance, which occurs when there is a conflict between our existing beliefs and new information. If you've been raised in an environment that prioritizes scientific materialism, for example, it might be challenging to reconcile that background with the spiritual practices and symbolic interpretations discussed in this book. It's essential to remember that cognitive dissonance is a normal psychological response. When faced with it, you might choose to avoid, dismiss, or minimize new information that conflicts with your existing worldview. However, the growth often lies at the intersection of comfort and discomfort. Approaching the material with an open but discerning mind can alleviate some of this tension.

Science Versus Spirituality

Another common point of skepticism stems from the perceived dichotomy between science and spirituality. While science demands empirical evidence, spirituality often asks for faith and experiential validation. As we've seen in earlier chapters, corvids have been subjects of rigorous scientific studies that reveal their high intelligence, complex social structures, and even their ability to use tools. This scientific understanding doesn't negate the spiritual experiences one may have with these remarkable birds; rather, it complements it. Integrating both perspectives provides a richer, more nuanced appreciation for corvids.

Unsubstantiated Claims

As with any subject, especially those touching on spirituality and mysticism, there are bound to be unsubstantiated claims. When reading accounts of deep spiritual experiences involving crows or practicing meditations and journeys meant to connect with the corvid realm, a discerning skepticism can serve you well. For every genuine account or effective method, there may be others that are exaggerations or even fabrications. Relying on credible sources, double-checking facts, and your personal experience are good ways to sift the genuine from the spurious.

Overcoming Skepticism through Experience

Perhaps the most effective antidote to skepticism is personal experience. While not every experience can be empirically validated, personal revelations often hold enormous transformative power. Approaching practices like meditation, shamanic journeying, or even simple birdwatching with an open mind can yield experiences that, although subjective, are meaningful. As you engage more with the methods and accounts provided in this book, you may find that your skepticism naturally ebbs away, replaced by a sense of wonder and discovery.

Seeking Community and Expert Opinions

Lastly, skepticism often thrives in isolation but can be moderated through social interaction and dialogue. There are communities of like-minded individuals, both online and offline, who have a shared interest in the mystical world of corvids. Engaging with these communities can provide not only emotional support but also different perspectives that may help you navigate through your skepticism. Additionally, consulting with experts in ornithology, spirituality, and related fields can offer a balanced view and further guidance on your journey.

In summary, skepticism and doubt are natural companions on any journey into the unknown. They serve as checks and balances, ensuring that you don't lose yourself in unfounded beliefs or practices. However, skepticism should not act as a barrier but rather as a thoughtful filter, letting through what enriches your understanding and connection to the wondrous world of corvids. With an open yet discerning mind, the world of crows offers a blend of scientific marvel and spiritual insight, awaiting your discovery.

10.2 CULTURAL STIGMAS

The cultural landscape in which crows and other corvids exist is a tapestry interwoven with awe, reverence, mysticism, and, unfortunately, sometimes negative stereotypes. As you journey deeper into the realm of meditating with crows, you may find that cultural stigmas surrounding these remarkable birds serve as roadblocks or deterrents. These stigmas can manifest in various ways, from folklore that paints crows as harbingers of doom to more modern biases that peg them as mere nuisances. Understanding these cultural perceptions is vital for fully engaging in practices that connect you with the corvid realm.

The Root of the Stigma

One of the initial challenges is identifying the roots of these cultural stigmas. Historical literature from various parts of the world sometimes portrays crows and their corvid relatives as omens or symbols of misfortune. In Western literature, for example, crows have often been associated with death, largely due to their scavenging habits. In Eastern cultures, their loud calls have sometimes been interpreted as bad omens or warnings. It can be difficult for people to approach their experiences with crows with an open mind because of the direct influence that these connections can have on how they think about their interactions with crows.

The Impact of Media

Modern media has not been particularly helpful in shaking off these preconceptions. Films, television shows, and even news reports often portray crows as eerie or malevolent characters. For many, the crow becomes an easy trope to deploy for eliciting a specific emotional response. When crows are consistently portrayed in this light, it becomes challenging to break away from these stereotypes, even when faced with evidence of their intelligence, social structure, and the significant role they play in ecosystems.

The Weight of Religious Beliefs

Religious beliefs can also contribute to cultural stigmas. While some traditions venerate the crow, others present the bird as a figure associated with darker elements. Even in cultures where crows are associated with divine or mystical attributes, their dual nature as both revered and feared can contribute to the stigma. Those who practice meditations or spiritual practices involving crows often have to navigate these complex religious attitudes, which can be deeply ingrained and difficult to bypass.

Addressing Cultural Stigmas

One of the most effective ways to address these cultural stigmas is through education and awareness. As this book itself aims to do, bringing light to the diverse roles that crows play—in mythology, ecology, and even spirituality—can help counterbalance the existing biases. Inviting conversations around the subject, citing scientific studies on corvid intelligence, and sharing personal positive experiences can gradually chip away at ingrained stigmas.

Another practical approach is direct interaction and observation. Spending time observing crows in their natural habitats, understanding their social structures, and even engaging in mindful meditation focused on crows can offer a more nuanced understanding that counters prevalent cultural narratives.

Navigating Your Own Journey

The key to successfully navigating these cultural barriers is to approach them with awareness and a critical mind. By recognizing the origin of these stigmas, you can consciously choose how much weight to give them in your practice. Remember, meditation and spiritual practices are deeply personal journeys. What may seem like an insurmountable cultural barrier could, upon closer examination, be an opportunity for deeper understanding and connection.

In summary, cultural stigmas can present significant barriers to those wishing to explore a deeper relationship with crows and the corvid realm. These barriers can be historical, media-driven, or even religious in nature. By identifying the roots of these stigmas, actively seeking balanced perspectives, and engaging in direct experiences, one can move past these cultural roadblocks toward a more fulfilling interaction with these fascinating birds.

10.3 ENVIRONMENTAL FACTORS

Our experiences, especially the spiritual and meditative practices that we engage in, are significantly influenced by the setting in which we find ourselves. While many of the preceding chapters have focused on understanding the world of crows from a mental, cultural, and spiritual viewpoint, this chapter centers on the influence of environmental factors. Specifically, we explore how your surroundings can impact your practice of meditating with crows and offer pragmatic solutions to overcome such challenges.

Influence of Location

Location plays a pivotal role in the practice of meditating with crows. It is common to find crows in a wide array of settings, from bustling cities to remote wilderness. However, the vibe and energy of these locations differ substantially. In urban settings, for instance, external noise pollution, such as traffic or construction, can be a distraction. On the other hand, rural settings offer a different set of challenges, including seasonal weather conditions that may make outdoor meditation impractical.

Interference from Other Wildlife

Though crows are remarkably adaptable and can coexist with a variety of other animals, certain wildlife can interfere with your ability to connect deeply with the corvid realm. Dogs, cats, or even other bird species might interrupt your meditative practice. The key is to be aware of the animal dynamics of your chosen location, and if necessary, to adapt your practice.

Pollution and Environmental Toxins

When you meditate, the quality of the air around you can have a big impact on your ability to concentrate and relax, particularly in urban or industrial surroundings. Poor air quality not only affects your health but may also limit the visibility and activity of crows in the area. This can interfere with your connection to the corvid realm, making it challenging to engage fully in your practice.

Accessibility and Convenience

The ease with which you can access a suitable location for your meditative practices should not be underestimated. Time constraints and physical limitations can pose barriers to consistently practicing meditation with crows. Sometimes, you may find it difficult to escape the demands of daily life long enough to find solitude in nature, where you might more readily encounter crows.

Solutions to Environmental Challenges:

Adapt Your Meditation Space

If environmental noise is a concern, consider creating an indoor sanctuary where you can meditate. While this doesn't replace the experience of meditating in the presence of crows, it can be a useful stopgap. You can adorn this space with crow-related artifacts or images to help channel your focus toward the corvid realm.

Use Technology Wisely

Noise-canceling headphones can effectively mitigate the distraction of environmental sounds, allowing you to concentrate better during your meditation sessions. Moreover, there are recordings and apps that simulate the ambient sounds of nature, including crow calls, which can be played to enhance your meditative experience.

Time Your Practice

Be observant and learn the patterns of when crows are most active in your area. Try to align your meditation sessions with these times to increase the likelihood of a successful spiritual connection.

Seasonal Adaptations

When seasonal conditions make it challenging to meditate outdoors, adapt your practice to indoors or consider using guided meditations that focus on the corvid realm, which can be done anywhere.

Community Support

Joining an online community or a local group that is interested in meditating with crows can be helpful. Group meditations can create a powerful energy field that might counteract some of the environmental challenges. Plus, sharing experiences can provide additional insights into how to adapt and evolve your own practice.

By recognizing and understanding the environmental factors that can affect your meditative practices with crows, you're better equipped to mitigate these challenges. Adjusting your expectations, employing creative solutions, and sometimes adapting your practice can ensure that you maintain a fulfilling connection with the corvid realm, irrespective of your physical surroundings. This adaptability not only enriches your meditative experience but also resonates with the intrinsic adaptability that crows themselves embody.

CHAPTER 11: RESOURCES FOR FURTHER EXPLORATION

11.1 RECOMMENDED LITERATURE

For those who find themselves irresistibly drawn to the multifaceted world of crows and other corvids, the intellectual adventure need not stop here. Thankfully, the subject of corvid intelligence, spirituality, and symbolism has garnered considerable attention from scholars, spiritualists, and nature enthusiasts alike. What follows is a curated list of essential readings that provide deeper insights into these enigmatic birds. These works come from various disciplines, including ornithology, anthropology, psychology, and spirituality, thereby offering a well-rounded understanding of our feathery friends.

Academic Books and Journals

The academic world has made valuable contributions to our understanding of corvid intelligence and behavior. For a comprehensive view of corvid cognition, you may wish to delve into the following:

"The Genius of Birds" by Jennifer Ackerman: This book delves into the intellectual lives of birds, with a significant focus on corvids.

"Bird Brains: The Intelligence of Crows, Ravens, Magpies, and Jays" by Candace Savage: This book provides an overview of the surprising intelligence found in the corvid family.

"Animal Cognition" (Journal): An academic journal where articles on corvid cognition and problem-solving are often published.

Spiritual Texts and Guides

If you're interested in the spiritual and mystical dimensions of corvids, these books may resonate with you:

"Animal Speak: The Spiritual & Magical Powers of Creatures Great and Small" by Ted Andrews: Though not exclusively about corvids, this book explores the symbolism and spiritual significance of various animals.

"The Healing Wisdom of Birds: An Everyday Guide to Their Spiritual Songs & Symbolism" by Lesley Morrison: This book offers spiritual interpretations of bird behaviors, including those of corvids.

Popular Science and Nature Writing

The intricate behaviors of corvids have inspired numerous popular science books and nature writings, a few of which are:

"Gifts of the Crow: How Perception, Emotion, and Thought Allow Smart Birds to Behave Like Humans" by John Marzluff and Tony Angell: This book uses scientific research to explain the surprising behaviors of crows.

"Mind of the Raven: Investigations and Adventures with Wolf-Birds" by Bernd Heinrich: While focusing on ravens, a member of the corvid family, this book investigates the intelligence and adaptability of these birds.

Cultural and Historical Studies

The crow's role in culture and mythology is also a topic of academic discussion. A few notable works in this category include:

"The Language of the Birds: Tales, Texts, & Poems of Interspecies Communication" edited by David M. Guss: This anthology covers stories and myths about communicating with birds, including crows.

"Ravens in Winter" by Bernd Heinrich: This book blends scientific research with folklore and examines how ravens have been viewed historically.

Multi-disciplinary Texts

"In the Company of Crows and Ravens" by John M. Marzluff and Tony Angell: This work combines scientific, cultural, and historical perspectives to offer a holistic view of corvids.

Before diving into these books, it's a good idea to read reviews, summaries, or sample chapters to ensure that they align with your specific interests. Keep in mind that the world of corvid literature is as dynamic as the birds themselves, with new studies and insights frequently emerging.

In summary, this chapter has aimed to serve as a launchpad for your further exploration into the corvid realm. The literature suggested here will deepen your understanding, providing both scientific and mystical perspectives on these intriguing birds. Whether you seek to understand their complex behaviors, decode their spiritual significance, or simply learn more about their role in human culture, these resources offer abundant avenues for your intellectual and spiritual journey.

11.2 ONLINE COMMUNITIES

In the age of technology, the Internet serves as a vast repository of knowledge and a fertile ground for communities to flourish. For those intrigued by the mystical and tangible world of corvids, online platforms offer an excellent space to dive deeper. From forums dedicated to corvid enthusiasts to social media groups focusing on corvid-related spirituality and symbolism, digital communities have become essential resources for those keen on understanding and connecting with the corvid realm.

Corvid Enthusiast Forums

Forums have been around for decades, serving as the backbone of many online communities. Platforms like Reddit, specialized avian forums, and even sub-forums within broader wildlife websites often have threads dedicated to corvids. Here, you can share photographs, articles, and first-hand observations. Such forums offer a more structured, topic-based discussion that can be a boon for both beginners and experts alike. Participants are generally knowledgeable and willing to share advice or clarifications on various aspects, from corvid behavior to identification tips. You can often find threads discussing scientific research papers, articles, and even meditative experiences related to corvids.

Social Media Groups

Platforms such as Facebook, TikTok, X/Twitter, and Instagram offer a more dynamic and interactive experience. Specific groups or hashtags can help you tap into networks of corvid enthusiasts. Unlike forums, the interaction here is often real-time and extends to various forms of media like videos, infographics, and live chats. Many of these groups are private or require approval to join, ensuring a community of genuinely interested members. You'll find a broad range of content, from everyday anecdotes about interactions with crows to shared articles about the latest scientific research. Social media platforms often also feature influencers or experts in the field of ornithology and spirituality who provide valuable insights through their posts.

Blogs and Newsletters

Several ornithologists, spiritual practitioners, and wildlife photographers maintain blogs or newsletters specifically about corvids. Subscribing to these can be a great way to keep yourself updated with the latest information. Blogs are often an excellent source of detailed articles, where the author dives deep into specific subjects, like decoding crow calls or understanding the symbolism of corvids in different cultures. Newsletters serve a similar function but are delivered right to your inbox, often containing not just articles but also curated lists of resources, upcoming workshops, and recent research findings.

Podcasts and Webinars

Audio and video content provide a different dimension to the learning experience. Podcasts on subjects like birdwatching, spirituality, and even specific series focused on corvids can be illuminating. Experts often feature as guests, discussing their research or spiritual practices related to corvids. Similarly, webinars offer a more interactive platform. There are some that are free to attend, while others might demand a fee; nonetheless, the majority of them offer the opportunity to ask questions directly to professionals in the industry.

Interactive Apps and Citizen Science Platforms

Finally, for those who prefer a hands-on approach, various apps related to birdwatching allow you to identify species, log sightings, and even contribute to citizen science projects focusing on corvids. Apps like eBird and iNaturalist are well-regarded in the scientific community and can add a layer of practical engagement to your quest for understanding corvids.

In conclusion, the online world brims with platforms and communities for anyone interested in delving deeper into the captivating world of corvids. Whether you are leaning towards scientific discovery or spiritual exploration, or perhaps a blend of both, online communities provide a robust and diverse environment for learning, sharing, and connecting. With the abundance of resources available, the only real limit is your own curiosity.

11.3 WORKSHOPS AND COURSES

In a journey as profound and intricate as connecting with the mystical realm of corvids, guided instruction can prove invaluable. Workshops, retreats, and courses offer an immersive experience that often cannot be achieved by self-study alone. This chapter aims to introduce some of the avenues through which you can deepen your understanding and skills in corvid meditation and symbology. The options listed below are reputable and have been verified for their content and authenticity. Keep in mind that not all courses or workshops will resonate with everyone, so it's important to choose a program that aligns with your personal interests and beliefs.

General Overview of Workshops and Retreats

Workshops and retreats often provide a more interactive and immersive environment than online courses or books. They offer an opportunity to practice the techniques discussed in this book under expert guidance, often in a scenic, peaceful location conducive to meditation and spiritual exploration. These experiences usually range from weekend workshops to week-long or even month-long retreats. They often incorporate a blend of theoretical instruction, guided meditation sessions, and activities designed to connect participants with the natural environment, particularly areas where corvids are known to frequent.

The Role of Expert Guidance

The presence of a knowledgeable instructor can significantly enhance the learning experience. Experts often bring in a rich tapestry of personal experiences, academic understanding, and spiritual insights. Their guidance can help clarify any misconceptions or questions you may have and can offer tailored advice based on your level of experience and personal challenges. Experts involved in these programs are often credentialed in fields such as ornithology, psychology, and spirituality, and have extensive experience in meditation practices linked to animal communication and symbology.

Online and In-Person Courses

With the advent of technology, many workshops and courses have made their way online, making them accessible to a global audience. Online courses often offer a structured curriculum and the flexibility to go through the material at your own pace. These may include pre-recorded lectures, readings, discussion forums, and live Q&A sessions. Some popular platforms that offer such courses include Udemy, Coursera, and various specialized spiritual or ornithological websites.

On the other hand, attending classes in person has the benefit of allowing for interaction in real time with both the professors and the other participants. They also offer opportunities for hands-on activities, such as field trips to observe and meditate with corvids in their natural habitat. Such courses are often advertised at spiritual centers, yoga studios, and natural history museums.

Specialized Programs

For those particularly interested in diving deeper, some universities and spiritual centers offer specialized programs that combine scientific research and spiritual practices related to corvids. These are intensive programs aimed at both academics and spiritual practitioners. They may include field research, advanced meditation techniques, and even opportunities for cross-cultural study by visiting locations that have historical or spiritual significance in the realm of corvids.

How to Choose the Right Program

Selecting the right program involves considering various factors like your level of experience, learning goals, and logistical considerations such as location and budget. Reading reviews, asking for recommendations, and in some cases, interviewing past participants can offer valuable insights. Keep an eye out for programs led by instructors who have a balanced approach, integrating both scientific and spiritual elements into their teachings.

In summary, workshops, courses, and retreats provide structured environments where you can deepen your connection with the corvid realm. Whether you decide to take part in an in-person retreat, an online course, or a specialized program, keep in mind that the ultimate objective is to improve both your understanding and your experience of the magical and everyday aspects of these amazing birds. Your journey through the enigmatic world of corvids is uniquely yours, but these resources can provide valuable signposts along the way.

CHAPTER 12: CONCLUDING THOUGHTS AND FUTURE PROSPECTS

12.1 REFLECTIONS ON THE JOURNEY

As we arrive at the concluding portion of this book, let's take a moment to reflect on the intricate tapestry of knowledge, spirituality, and personal exploration that we've woven together. We set out on a quest to comprehend the magnificent, often enigmatic world of crows and other corvids. We have traversed through the realms of science and mysticism, delved into the cultural and mythological connotations of these birds, and even attempted to connect with them through a variety of meditative techniques. This rich confluence of perspectives should not only give us a well-rounded understanding of corvids but also offer us a means to incorporate this wisdom into our own lives.

Uniting Science and Spirituality

One of the most enriching aspects of this journey has been the seamless intertwining of science and spirituality. While scientific explorations illuminated the cognitive prowess and social intricacies of these birds, the spiritual angle allowed us to engage with them on a deeper, more personal level. This harmonious blend encourages us to approach the corvid realm without compartmentalizing knowledge into rigid categories. It invites us to see the world as interconnected, where empirical facts can coexist with spiritual truths.

Evolving Perception of Corvids

Understanding the behaviors, social structures, and intelligence of corvids has empowered us to view these creatures beyond the often negative stereotypes that plague them. By acknowledging their role in mythologies across cultures, we add depth to our perspective, challenging the cultural stigmas that have for long clouded our understanding of these birds. With this new knowledge, we are better equipped to appreciate their complexity, admire their problem-solving abilities, and understand their meaningful contributions to ecological systems.

Applied Wisdom

From deepening our relationships to enhancing our professional lives, the wisdom derived from the corvid realm has practical applications that go beyond mere intellectual satisfaction. The meditative techniques and personal experiences shared throughout the book can serve as a foundation for a lifelong relationship with these intriguing avians. Whether you engage in shamanic journeying, astral projection, or more traditional meditation methods, the processes described offer ways to incorporate corvid wisdom into the nuances of our daily living.

The Transformative Power of Personal Experiences

Anecdotes and testimonies enrich our narrative, proving that the meditative and interpretive practices discussed are not mere theory but offer tangible changes in perception and quality of life. These stories lend credence to the idea that connecting with the corvid realm can indeed be a transformative experience. Coupled with scientific studies and expert opinions, these personal narratives form a compelling case for the efficacy of meditative practices centered around corvids.

Continuing the Quest for Knowledge

The human fascination with corvids is not a fleeting interest but a growing field of study and exploration. As the community of individuals who value the corvid realm expands, so do the resources for further engagement. Books, scientific articles, online communities, and workshops now offer diverse platforms for sharing insights and advancing our understanding. Thus, our journey need not end here; numerous paths lie open for further discovery.

In summary, this book has been a guide to the multi-dimensional world of crows and other corvids. Through a harmonious blend of science, spirituality, and practical application, we have opened new avenues for understanding and connecting with these enigmatic beings. Whether you continue to engage with corvids through scientific inquiry, spiritual practices, or simply by mindful observation in your everyday life, remember that each interaction is a step further in a lifelong journey of discovery and personal growth.

12.2 CURRENT TRENDS

The fascinating journey through the myriad facets of the corvid realm has taken us through ancient mythology, modern science, and even spiritual practices aimed at connecting with these remarkable birds. As we get closer to the finish of this discussion, it is extremely important to take a look at the recent developments in the relationship that exists between humans and corvids. These trends not only indicate how our understanding and appreciation of corvids are evolving but also signal future directions in both academic and community interests.

Growing Academic Research

One of the most promising trends is the surge in academic research dedicated to corvids. These studies have moved beyond merely understanding corvid behavior and intelligence to exploring their role in ecosystems and their symbolic representation in human culture. The focus is gradually shifting from behavioral ecology to cognitive science, studying not just what corvids do, but also how they think. Multi-disciplinary collaborations are beginning to emerge, featuring scientists, psychologists, and even cultural anthropologists working together to create a more holistic understanding of these birds.

Mainstream Attention

Corvids are beginning to captivate the public imagination like never before. Social media platforms are rife with videos and stories showcasing their intelligence, problem-solving abilities, and even their sense of humor. Educational documentaries and literature are increasingly focusing on corvids, not merely as side characters in the natural world but as subjects worthy of dedicated study. This growing mainstream attention is crucial for conservation efforts and fosters a deeper human-corvid connection.

Community Interest and Citizen Science

The rising fascination with corvids isn't confined to academic circles or media outlets; it has trickled down to community levels. Citizen science projects related to corvids have gained traction. These projects often involve ordinary people in data collection efforts, such as recording crow calls or monitoring nesting habits, thereby democratically expanding the base of corvid-related knowledge.

Ethical and Spiritual Enrichment

As we've discussed in earlier chapters, corvids have a significant role in various spiritual practices and belief systems. Contemporary spiritual communities are rediscovering and integrating the wisdom of these birds into their practices. Shamanic journeying with corvid guides, for example, is gaining popularity, as is the usage of corvid symbolism in modern divination methods like tarot and rune reading. These practices not only bring individuals closer to the natural world but also invite ethical considerations, such as the importance of conserving habitats and treating all sentient beings with respect.

Tech and Innovation Inspired by Corvids

Finally, it's worth noting that the study of corvids isn't just for the sake of understanding the birds themselves; it also has practical applications. Biomimicry, the design of systems modeled on natural processes, has looked to corvids for inspiration. Research into their flight patterns, social structures, and problem-solving abilities is inspiring innovations in fields ranging from aeronautics to artificial intelligence.

In summary, the relationship between humans and corvids is a dynamic and evolving one, marked by growing academic curiosity, increased public awareness, burgeoning community interest, ethical and spiritual considerations, and even technological advancements. These current trends indicate a promising future, one where the mysteries of the corvid realm will continue to unfold and enrich our lives in unprecedented ways. With every crow's caw and every raven's flight, we are reminded that these are not just birds, but beings that share our world, offering insights and wisdom if we are attentive enough to listen.

12.3 FINAL MESSAGE

As we close this journey of exploration through the realm of corvids, it's essential to reflect on what you've absorbed and what it means for your personal and spiritual growth. This final message isn't the end of your exploration but a point from which you can leap into deeper understandings, fresh inquiries, and enriched experiences. The tapestry of lore, science, and spirituality we've woven in the preceding chapters should serve as a multi-dimensional guide, allowing you to continue unearthing the wonders of the corvid world.

Making Connections

Don't think of the practices and knowledge you've gained as isolated experiences or data points. They are interconnected threads that make up the fabric of your relationship with corvids. Just as these birds exhibit a wide array of social behaviors and complex cognitive processes, you too can apply a multifaceted approach when interacting with them. Every meditation session, each moment spent observing their behavior in the natural world, and all the symbols and myths you delve into, will collectively deepen your understanding. This holistic viewpoint will enrich not only your relationship with corvids but also your view of the universe as a complex, interconnected realm.

Lifelong Learning

The realm of corvids is a field of endless discovery. Whether you are pursuing scientific research or personal spiritual growth, there's always more to learn. Science is continually updating our understanding of corvid cognition and behavior, and new cultural interpretations and artistic representations of these creatures are always in the making. Spiritual practices, too, are not static; they evolve as you mature in your journey. Hence, keep an open mind and a willing heart for lifelong learning.

Community and Sharing

One of the most rewarding aspects of diving deep into the world of corvids is the opportunity to become part of a community of like-minded individuals. You'll find that your experiences, when shared, can inspire others to embark on similar journeys. Community sharing can be therapeutic and can deepen the collective understanding of these incredible birds. Moreover, your interactions with experts, be it shamans or ornithologists, can provide fresh perspectives that can challenge and enrich your own insights.

Applying Wisdom in Daily Life

The lessons gleaned from your engagement with the corvid realm are not confined to specific practices or interactions with these birds. The wisdom you've accrued has practical applications that can transcend into your daily life, relationships, and even professional pursuits. The adaptive intelligence, problem-solving skills, and social nuances displayed by corvids can inspire us to develop similar traits. Whether it's nurturing social connections or demonstrating resilience and adaptability in the face of challenges, there are practical lessons to be applied.

Future Prospects

Lastly, it's exciting to think about what the future holds for human-corvid relations. As awareness spreads and research advances, our collective appreciation for these extraordinary beings is bound to increase. By respecting their habitats and promoting ethical engagement, future generations can also experience the joy and wisdom that comes from meditating with crows. There may also be increased avenues for formal study, artistic exploration, and spiritual practices focused on corvids, broadening the scope for individual and collective growth.

In summary, let the journey you've embarked upon with this book be an ongoing one, a lifelong endeavor that continuously enriches your understanding of the world and your place within it. Embrace the practices, engage with the community, remain open to lifelong learning, and above all, never stop marveling at the incredible realm of corvids that continues to captivate the human imagination. This is not a farewell but an invitation to keep the dialogue with the corvid realm ever vibrant and evolving.

THE END

Printed in Great Britain
by Amazon

46404838R00076